WESTERN MOVIE
WIT & WISDOM

WESTERN MOVIE
WIT & WISDOM

JIM KANE

TOPIC ILLUSTRATIONS BY ISABEL LASATER HERNANDEZ

BRIGHT SKY PRESS

DEDICATION

To the memory of my father and mother, Harold and Eleanor, and my brother, Edward; to sisters Janie, Nancy and Mary Beth; to my lovely, supportive wife, Vickie; and to my wonderful adult children, Jennifer and Michael.

CONTENTS

For a complete bibliography of movie titles, please visit www.brightskypress.com.

INTRODUCTION

When Lucy Laughton asked Ernest Albright if he had any hobbies outside his optometry business, he quipped:

Ernest: The West.
Lucy: The West?
Ernest: The Wild West.
Lucy: Oh, that West. What do you do with it?
Ernest: I don't do anything with it. I sort of carry it around in here [pointing to self].
Lucy Laughton played by Patricia Clarkson and Ernest Albright played by Judge Reinhold in Four Eyes and Six-Guns *(1992)*

And that's pretty much what I do. I loved watching westerns as a kid. I couldn't get enough of them. During the last fifteen years or so, I began taping westerns on television and categorizing quotations from them. I would find myself making reference to a western quotation at work or play. I would catch myself blurting out to a co-worker, "No point in feeling every bump in the road." *Mustang Country (1976)*; or in my personal life, "When you're faced with a choice, go after the best of both." *Banjo Hackett: Roamin' Free (1976)*.

Efforts to define westerns within a time or place have been pointless. The conventional wisdom places the period from 1865–1900 in an area west of the Mississippi. But before that ink dried, there was North to Alaska (1960), Last of the Mohicans (1920), Quigley Down Under (1990), Hud (1963), and hundreds more, that shot those boundaries out of the saddle. No, the western exists elsewhere:

Being out in the world is a state of mind, not of geography.
Rupert Venneker played by Peter Ustinov in The Sundowners *(1960)*

But the western is much more than a state of mind. The western lives in our hearts as well:

Wherever they get to, all good stories begin and end in the same place. And that's the heart of a man or a woman.
Narration by Wilford Brimley in <u>Last of the Dogmen</u> (1995)

And as far as truth is concerned, who cares!

Most of what follows is true.
Prologue in <u>Butch Cassidy and the Sundance Kid</u> (1969)

Just because it's a tall tale don't mean it ain't true.
Jonas Hackett played by Stephen Lang in <u>Tall Tale</u> (1995)

What follows here is not intended to be an accurate re-creation of historical fact ... not that it matters.
Prologue in <u>The Last Ride of the Dalton Gang</u> (1979)

Maybe this isn't the way it was ... it's the way it should have been.
Prologue in <u>The Life and Times of Judge Roy Bean</u> (1972)

So saddle up and hit the trail for some cowboy humor, entertainment, and quirkiness!

If there's one place in this old world where a cowboy can kick off his spurs and be happy for the rest of his life, that's where we're going. So hang on, partner!
Ross Bodine played by William Holden in <u>Wild Rovers</u> (1971)

We better get aboard. I have an idea this is going to be a very interesting trip.
Wild Bill Hickok played by Bill Elliott in <u>Hands Across the Rockies</u> (1941)

ABILITY

We all got things we can't do and things we can.
Joshua Cabe played by Dan Dailey in <u>The Daughters of Joshua Cabe Return</u> (1975)

ACCEPTANCE

If you can't accept me the way I am, you'll never be happy with me.
Belle Starr played by Elizabeth Montgomery in <u>Belle Starr</u> (1980)

When you're in love with someone, you don't try to change them. You take them the way they are.
Jo played by Rhonda Fleming in <u>Gun Glory</u> (1957)

You got to take things for what they are.
Big Eli Wakefield played by Burt Lancaster in <u>The Kentuckian</u> (1955)

A lot of things you just got to ride away from.
Country Boy played by Richard Rust in <u>The Legend of Tom Dooley</u> (1959)

Nika: You never let anything get to you. You just take it as it comes.
Dan: When you've been around as long as I have, you'll get the hang of it. No point in feeling every bump in the road.
Nika played by Nika Mina and Dan played by Joel McCrea in <u>Mustang Country</u> (1976)

The sooner you learn to accept the fact that we're here to stay, the better off you'll be.
Ann Howard played by Phyllis Planchard in The Westward Trail (1948)

ACCIDENTS

Gus: It's an accident she's even on this trip!
Clara: Well, I never noticed you having accidents with ugly girls.
Gus McCrae played by Robert Duvall and Clara Allen played by Angelica Huston in Lonesome Dove (1989)

ACCOMPLISHMENT

A man gets halfway, he ought to have something of his own, something to belong to, be proud of.
Sam Boone played by Pernell Roberts in Ride Lonesome (1959)

ACCOUNTABILITY

I've never worn a coat of whitewash yet, and I won't start now.
Captain Nathan Brittles played by John Wayne in She Wore a Yellow Ribbon (1949)

ACTIONS

It doesn't really matter who you are; it's what you're doing that counts.
Christella played by Coleen Gray in Arrow in the Dust (1954)

After all any man says, it's what he does that counts.
Hooker played by Gary Cooper in Garden of Evil (1954)

Your actions may have consequences for everybody.
Brian Athlone played by Don Wycherley in One Man's Hero (1999)

Actions speak louder than words.
Doc Holliday played by Walter Huston in The Outlaw (1943)

ADAPTATION

If you can't fix it, Jack, you gotta stand it.
Ennis Del Mar played by Heath Ledger in <u>Brokeback Mountain</u> *(2005)*

Sometimes you just gotta roll with what's thrown at ya.
Print Ritter played by Robert Duvall in <u>Broken Trail</u> *(2006)*

You know, I lived through eight prisons and about the same amount of wives by just blending into the background when the noise gets loud.
Frank Taggert played by Arthur Hunnicutt in <u>Devil's Canyon</u> *(1953)*

Some things fit into what they are, and some to what they've been taught.
Bless Keough played by Jeffrey Hunter in <u>Gun for a Coward</u> *(1957)*

ADO

Dillon: You're making a lot out of nothing.
Marshal: You're not making enough of it.
Dillon played by George Mathews and Marshal Cass Silver played by Robert Ryan in <u>The Proud Ones</u> *(1956)*

ADOLESCENCE

He's between hay and grass.
Matt Dillon played by James Arness in <u>Gunsmoke: One Man's Justice</u> *(1994)*

ADVANTAGE

Even if you have a small advantage, be careful not to lose it.
Cacopoulos played by Eli Wallach in <u>Ace High</u> *(1967)*

ADVERSITY

Faith alone will not dig us out of it. We will need courage in our hearts and shovels in our hands.
The Minister played by Russell Simpson in <u>Three Faces West</u> *(1940)*

ADVICE

I don't take advice. I give it!
Wheat played by Earl Holliman in <u>Alias Smith and Jones</u> (1971)

Only fools and jackasses bray advice.
Zack Hollister played by Brian Bloom in <u>Brotherhood of the Gun</u> (1991)

Is there anything else you want to tell me that I already know?
Marshal Curly Wilcox played by Johnny Cash in <u>Stagecoach</u> (1986)

AFFORDABILITY

I make it a point to never smoke a cigar that I can't afford.
Hunt Lawton played by Burt Reynolds in <u>Johnson County War</u> (2001)

AFTERWORLD

Man's knowledge is very small, life is very great, and the mysteries are immense—and the hereafter is profoundly long lasting.
Preacher Bob played by Peter Boyle in <u>Kid Blue</u> (1973)

Through the Toll Gate that bars the Portal of Tomorrow and inexorably claims tribute for the Sins of Yesterday.
Caption in <u>The Toll Gate</u> (1920)

AGENDA

What's on your mind and how much is it going to cost me?
Ike Slant played by Slim Pickens in <u>An Eye for an Eye</u> (1966)

AGING

Time ain't exactly a beauty treatment.
Jim Sherwood played by Brian Donlevy in <u>Billy the Kid</u> (1941)

Nobody has got much use for an old man.
Mister played by Ben Johnson in <u>Bite the Bullet</u> (1975)

I may be old as dirt but I ain't in it!
Jim Valesky played by Larry Mahan in <u>Blood Trail</u> (1997)

I feel like I'm standing in a puddle of sand and it's all just drifting away.
Wild Bill Hickock played by Frederic Forest in <u>Calamity Jane</u> (1984)

Henry: Maybe I am a little afraid of growing old. What's wrong with that?
Jenny: Nothing. So am I. I just thought there was a chance we could do it together.
Henry played by James Brolin and Jenny played by Sally Kirkland in <u>Cheatin' Hearts</u> (1993)

A man's no older than he feels.
Hopalong Cassidy played by William Boyd in <u>The Frontiersmen</u> (1938)

I think the older I get, the better I used to be.
Brady Hawkes played by Kenny Rogers in <u>Gambler V: Playing for Keeps</u> (1994)

At my age, you learn a new name and you gotta forget an old one.
Wesley Birdsong played by Gordon Tootoosis in <u>Lone Star</u> (1996)

The years don't make wisdom, they just make old age. One can be young in years and old in hours.
Jack Beauregard played by Henry Fonda in <u>My Name Is Nobody</u> (1973)

Time's been tailing us and it overtook us!
Nash Crawford played by Walter Brennan in <u>The Over-the-Hill Gang</u> (1969)

I was wrong in thinking that a new suit and a fresh shave could take me back twenty years.
The Baltimore Kid played by Fred Astaire in <u>The Over-the-Hill Gang Rides Again</u> (1970)

Sooner or later, it comes your turn. Because if you live, you get older. And if you live long enough, you get old.
Clay Lomax played by Gregory Peck in <u>Shoot Out</u> (1971)

When I was your age, it was mostly girls. Now at my age, it's mostly that it mostly ain't.
Whitey played by Douglas Fowley in These Thousand Hills (1959)

I believe like Cicero did: you must begin to be an old man early if you want to
be an old man long.
Swiftwater Tilton played by Adolphe Menjou in Timberjack (1955)

AGITATION

He's just stirring things up to see what floats to the top.
Nick Evers played by Roddy McDowall in 5 Card Stud (1968)

It's easy to keep the pot boiling once it's started.
Pecos Jack Anthony played by Kenneth Thomson in Hopalong Cassidy (1935)

ALLEGIANCE

A man can't live alone. He must have allegiance to a people, to a nation.
O'Meara played by Rod Steiger in Run of the Arrow (1957)

ALTERNATIVES

You do not have to stop force. It is easier to redirect it. Learn more ways to
preserve rather than destroy. Avoid rather than check; check rather than hurt;
hurt rather than maim; maim rather than kill. For all life is precious; nor can
any be replaced.
Master Kan played by Philip Ahn in Kung Fu (1972)

AMBITION

Judge: I take it for granted, Bill, that you'll be the mayor.
Trigger Bill: Who, me? Oh, no, I don't want any honors for meself. I just want
to own the town.
*Jackson Douglas played by Lewis Stone and Trigger Bill played by Wallace Beery in
The Bad Man of Brimstone (1937)*

Sometimes a little ambition makes people see dirt when there isn't any.
Lt. Jed Sayre played by Audie Murphy in <u>*Column South*</u> *(1953)*

I don't intend to start at the bottom. Been there ... too crowded.
Haven played by Dick Powell in <u>*Station West*</u> *(1948)*

AMERICA

Blake: Why do you have this [gun]?
Russell: This is America.
William Blake played by Johnny Depp and Thel Russell played by Mili Avital in <u>*Dead Man*</u> *(1996)*

Tucson: You know, there used to be a time when being an American meant something.
Stony: It still does. It stands for freedom and fair play.
Tucson Smith played by Ray Corrigan and Stony Brooke played by John Wayne in <u>*The Night Riders*</u> *(1939)*

AMPUTATION

Woodrow: What do you want legs for anyway? You don't like to do nothing but sit on the porch and drink whiskey.
Gus: I like to kick a pig every once in awhile. How would I do that?
Captain Woodrow F. Call played by Tommy Lee Jones and Gus McCrae played by Robert Duvall in <u>*Lonesome Dove*</u> *(1989)*

ANARCHY

Unenforced law is an invitation to anarchy.
Frank Canton played by Sam Waterston in <u>*Heaven's Gate*</u> *(1980)*

ANGER

Don't heat up so fast, boy. It makes you boil over.
Tom Earley played by Stewart Granger in <u>*Gun Glory*</u> *(1957)*

Lesson number one: never attack in anger.
Don Diego de la Vega/Zorro played by Anthony Hopkins in <u>The Mask of Zorro</u> (1998)

ANIMALS

They say the best way to control an animal is to be a little smarter than he is.
Jason Sweet played by Glenn Ford in <u>The Sheepman</u> (1958)

ANNOYANCE

You're getting to be a burr under my saddle!
Jim Bowie played by James Arness in <u>The Alamo: Thirteen Days to Glory</u> (1987)

ANSWERS

A person has got to find his own answers.
Mrs. "Ma" Callum played by Judith Anderson in <u>Pursued</u> (1947)

ANTICIPATION

Nothing is ever so worthwhile as it seems beforehand.
Cherry Malotte played by Marlene Dietrich in <u>The Spoilers</u> (1942)

The worst ain't so bad when it finally happens. Not half as bad as you figure it'll be before it's happened.
Bob Curtin played by Tim Holt in <u>The Treasure of the Sierra Madre</u> (1948)

APOLOGY

Always permit a woman to apologize if she insists upon it. It makes her feel better and noble.
Padre José played by Pedro de Cordoba in <u>Range War</u> (1939)

APPEARANCES

You're a sight for sore eyes!
Fuzzy Jones played by Al St. John in <u>Billy the Kid in Texas</u> (1940)

Some men are handsome. So is a diamondback rattlesnake.
Stella played by Ruth Brennan in <u>California Passage</u> (1950)

Things are not always what they seem.
Roy Rogers as himself in <u>Eyes of Texas</u> (1948)

Sometimes things can look one way and turn out to be altogether something else.
Celia Gray played by Virginia Mayo in <u>Fort Dobbs</u> (1958)

Still waters run deep.
Dusty Cosgrove played by Pat Buttram in <u>Hills of Utah</u> (1951)

Sometimes polishing your britches gets you further than blistering your feet.
The Lone Ranger played by Clayton Moore in <u>The Lone Ranger</u> (1956)

People aren't always what they seem.
The Sheriff played by Lane Chandler in <u>Quantrill's Raiders</u> (1958)

Never judge a heifer by the flick of her tail.
Jim Curry played by Earl Holliman in <u>The Rainmaker</u> (1956)

Just because I'm rough and dirty, and don't wear underwear, don't mean that I ain't artistic.
Pop McGovern played by Dub Taylor in <u>The Shakiest Gun in the West</u> (1968)

APPETITE

A one-armed man eats as much as a man with two arms.
Mike Evans played by Bill Williams in <u>The Cariboo Trail</u> (1950)

APPLES

A rotten apple spoils the barrel.
John Riley played by Tom Berenger in <u>One Man's Hero</u> (1999)

APPRECIATION

Now if you want only one thing too much, it's likely to turn out a disappointment. Now the only healthy way to live, as I see it, is to learn to like all the little, everyday things.
Gus McCrae played by Robert Duvall in Lonesome Dove (1989)

You know what they say, honey: you don't miss your water until your well runs dry.
Rose played by Helen Shaver in Pair of Aces (1990)

ARGUMENTS

I like a good argument. It clears the air for other things.
Mrs. Waynebrook played by Verna Felton in The Oklahoman (1957)

I never heard an argument that was worth a man's life.
Terrall Butler played by James Mitchell in The Peacemaker (1956)

There's always two sides to every argument.
Montana Smith played by Noah Beery in The Tulsa Kid (1940)

ARMY

There's no room for sentiment in the Army.
General Braxton Bragg played by John Doucette in Journey to Shiloh (1968)

Napoleon made the profound observation that an army travels on its stomach.
William Quantrill played by Brain Donlevy in Kansas Raiders (1950)

Sometimes I wonder if the Army really needs Second Lieutenants.
Colonel Jeb Britten played by Bruce Bennett in The Last Outpost (1951)

He wasn't born. He was issued!
Olaf Swenson played by Alan Hale, Jr., in The Man Behind the Gun (1952)

The Army doesn't need men who think they're indispensable.
Lt. Colonel Unger played by Forrest Tucker in <u>Oh! Susanna</u> (1951)

The Army is my home, and I will protect my home with my life.
Master Sergeant Henry J. Foggers played by Claude Akins in <u>Waterhole #3</u> (1967)

ARRANGEMENTS

Rev: There are occasional evenings when I get very lonely, Miss Starr. If there were an agreement between you and me, an arrangement of some kind, an understanding if you know what I mean. What I'm trying to say....
Belle: You've already said it, Preacher. I get your meaning. You're stumbling around trying to find a Christian way to propose an un-Christian thing.
Rev. Meeks played by Geoffrey Lewis and Belle Starr played by Elizabeth Montgomery in <u>Belle Starr</u> (1980)

ARREST

Hands on the table! Right one first. That's the one with the thumb on the left.
Sheriff John Whaley played by Robert Vaughn in <u>Desperado</u> (1987)

Dub: Well, ain't you going to arrest him or something?
Deputy: Dub, that man rode into town trailing three corpses. And he just accounted for two more, and it ain't even noon yet. You arrest him!
Dub was uncredited and Deputy Rudd played by Jim Beaver in <u>Gunsmoke: To the Last Man</u> (1992)

ASSISTANTS

Titus: I'm curious. What do you expect to achieve with such crass ineptitude, such utter incompetence, such colossal stupidity?
Milford: Well, I was hoping to become your assistant.
Titus Queasley played by Will Wright and Milford Farnsworth played by Bob Hope in <u>Alias Jesse James</u> (1959)

ASSOCIATION

You can't rub up against dirt and not get some of it on you.
Jed Kilton played by Richard Arlen in <u>The Big Bonanza</u> (1944)

A man is judged according to the herd he trails with.
Robert "Buck" Sawyer played by Tom Keene in <u>Sundown Trail</u> (1931)

ASTUTE

Oliver: You're very astute.
Nugget: Is that good?
Oliver: That means you're smart.
Nugget: You're a fine judge of character, Oliver.
Oliver Budge played by Gene Roth and Nugget Clark played by Eddy Waller in <u>Oklahoma Badlands</u> (1948)

ATHEIST

Maybe I'm like the perfect atheist. Sometimes I even got to doubt my own disbelief.
Marla played by Linda Kozlowski in <u>Shaughnessy</u> (1996)

AUTHORITY

When you give a man authority, you can't tie his hands behind him.
Asa Wentworth played by George Cleveland in <u>Sunset in Wyoming</u> (1941)

AVOIDANCE

When you're grown up, you'll find out that there are certain things you can't stay out of.
Tom Earley played by Stewart Granger in <u>Gun Glory</u> (1957)

BABY

Why didn't your mother eat you when you were born?
The Cisco Kid played by Jimmy Smits in <u>The Cisco Kid</u> (1994)

BACHELOR

Nobody can be a bachelor too long.
Chico played by J. Carrol Naish in <u>The Kissing Bandit</u> (1948)

BACK STABBING

I don't mind what people say behind my back as long as they don't say it to my face.
Scotty McQuade played by Tom Tyler in <u>Rip Roarin' Buckaroo</u> (1936)

BACKBONE

Someday I hope you can grow a backbone.
John Banner played by Dale Robertson in <u>Dakota Incident</u> (1956)

BACKGROUND CHECK

The way things were, I needed a fast gun more than a clean bill of health.

Sheriff Henry Plummer played by Marshal Reed in <u>The Wild Westerner</u> (1962)

BACKING AWAY

There are some things a man can't back away from.
Carl Avery played by Barton MacLane in <u>Noose for a Gunman</u> (1960)

A man can only back away so long.
Steve Fallon played by Richard Basehart in <u>The Savage Guns</u> (1961)

BACKYARDS

You can't rely on Washington to make peace in your own backyard. This is one of those things you got to do yourself.
Marshal Will Kane played by Tom Skerritt in <u>High Noon</u> (2000)

BAD GUY

He's the kind of a fellow who'd kill ya for two bits and give you back twenty cents change.
Pecos played by Tom Tyler in <u>Cheyenne</u> (1947)

BAD PENNY

A bad penny always turns up.
Zeb Calloway played by Arthur Hunnicutt in <u>The Big Sky</u> (1952)

BADGES

This badge is a magic piece of metal. Evil men fear it, decent men respect it.
Marshal Matt Brennan played by Douglas Fowley in <u>The Badge of Marshal Brennan</u> (1957)

People ought to respect the badge and not the gun behind it.
Tom Brewster played by Will Rogers, Jr., in <u>The Boy from Oklahoma</u> (1954)

We need some tin showing around here!
Sig Evers played by Denver Pyle in <u>5 Card Stud</u> (1968)

Remember that badge of his don't die. It just gets up and comes after you again on the shirt pocket of another man.
Sheriff Klacaden played by Charles Kemper in <u>Gunfighters</u> (1947)

It ain't only a badge you're carrying. It's your reputation.
Sheriff Buck Weston played by Fess Parker in <u>The Hangman</u> (1959)

It looks like this pin is a little too heavy for you, sonny.
Alex Flood played by Dean Martin in <u>Rough Night in Jericho</u> (1967)

BANKS

Clumhill: This bank is not in the habit of lending money to people who are broke.
Mabel: Who else needs it?
Clumhill played by Charles Halton and Mabel King played by Joan Davis in <u>The Traveling Saleswoman</u> (1950)

BARBED WIRE

Folks say the west was conquered by the railroad. My daddy says it was conquered by barbed wire.
Eileen Spenser played by Andie MacDowell in <u>Bad Girls</u> (1994)

It has always been my contention that if a man has the right to lock his front door, he has the right to wire around his field.
Cash Karger played by Wallis Clark in <u>Forbidden Trail</u> (1932)

BARBERS

Nobody knows a town, or the people in it, like the town barber.
Allan "Rocky" Lane played by himself in <u>Savage Frontier</u> (1953)

BARK & BITE

His bark is much worse than his bite.
Mary played by Pauline Moore in <u>Days of Jesse James</u> (1939)

BARTENDER

I don't drink. I'm studying to be a bartender.
Latigo played by John Day in <u>Night Passage</u> (1957)

BATHING

Grandpa, when you take your first bath, don't skip your mind.
Private Robert Travis played by John Russell in <u>Fort Massacre</u> (1958)

Hot water and a tub go well together, especially when they surround a beautiful woman.
Nathan Stark played by Robert Ryan in <u>The Tall Men</u> (1955)

BATTERED WOMEN

The trouble with beatings is that you get used to them. They become like everything else, something to be gotten through like a sack of dirty clothes.
Maria played by Betta St. John in <u>The Naked Dawn</u> (1955)

BEAN, JUDGE ROY

Justifiable homicide. I fine that man two bits for firing a gun in a public building [comment following killing drunk for shooting bullet hole in picture of Lily Langtry]. I also fine him $52 for lying around [comment upon counting money in a dead drunk's pocket].
Judge Roy Bean played by Paul Newman in <u>The Life and Times of Judge Roy Bean</u> (1972).

BEAUTY

Fiske: I've found that pretty women speak the same language all over the world.
Hooker: What about the ugly ones?
Fiske: I never listened.
Fiske played by Richard Widmark and Hooker played by Gary Cooper in <u>Garden of Evil</u> (1954)

Every creature has its rightful place. And in its rightful place, it becomes beautiful.
Archie Grey Owl played by Pierce Brosnan in <u>Grey Owl</u> (1999)

Buteo: There are some who find beauty in the most bleak surroundings.

Zack: You know, now I know why I needed you. I'd never be able to come up with all these pointless and oblique philosophies by my lonesome.

Buteo played by Jimmie F. Skaggs and Zack Stone played by Richard Joseph Paul in <u>Oblivion</u> *(1994)*

A thing of beauty is a joy forever.

Riley played by J.M. Kerrigan, quoting John Keats, in <u>The Silver Whip</u> *(1953)*

That is the trouble with things that are too beautiful. Too often they must be shut away where people cannot see them.

Don Lopez played by Harry Vejar in <u>West to Glory</u> *(1947)*

BELIEFS

One can do many things when one believes in the final outcome.

Jeanne Dubois played by Nicole Maurey in <u>The Jayhawkers</u> *(1959)*

A man believes what he wants to believe.

Richard Connor played by Peter Lawford in <u>Kangaroo</u> *(1952)*

Are you going to believe what you see or what I tell you?

George Washington McLintock played by John Wayne in <u>McLintock!</u> *(1963)*

You don't want to always believe what you hear, only half of what you see.

Sam McCloud played by Dennis Weaver in <u>The Return of Sam McCloud</u> *(1989)*

BEST INTEREST

People don't always do what's best for them.

Jennie Reed played by Lee Purcell in <u>The Gambler</u> *(1980)*

BETTING

Lila: I suspect you're a gambling man.

Ben: Would you like to bet on it?

Lila Gates was uncredited and Ben Maverick played by Charles Frank in <u>Young Maverick</u> (1979)

BETWIXT & BETWEEN

It looks like you're caught between the sap and the bark.

Will Penny played by Charlton Heston in <u>Will Penny</u> (1968)

BI-RACIAL

It will not be easy. But those of us with twin roots sometimes become the strongest trees.

Kwai Chang Caine played by David Carradine in <u>Kung Fu: The Movie</u> (1986)

BIBLES

Now in addition to the Ecclesiastics, never forget what your grandfather used to say. Grandmother would question, 'Why do you carry your gun if it is written whether or not you are to die?' Grandfather would answer, 'I carry it just in case it's written the other one shall die.'

Jeremiah Sanchez played by Jorge Rivero in <u>Bordello</u> (1979)

Duchess: The Bible tells us that he who doeth what is good and doeth what is holy is going to doeth all right.

Mormon Wife: Where is that in the Bible?

Duchess: Under the doeth's.

Duchess/Amanda Quaid played by Goldie Hawn and the Mormon Wife was uncredited in <u>The Duchess and the Dirtwater Fox</u> (1976)

You got the right to hear a few words from a preacher. Unfortunately, our preacher is out of town. But, luckily, we got Farley McLard here. He's a feed and grain salesman, and he owns a Bible.

The Posse Leader played by Jeff Corey in <u>The Gun and the Pulpit</u> (1974)

BIBLE BELT

They knowed their Bible as well as they knowed their own names. If they didn't, they got the tar licked out of 'em!
Ma McDade played by Jo Van Fleet in <u>The King and Four Queens</u> (1956)

BIG

Just remember what I told you: think big, act big, and you'll be big.
Big Jack Mahoney played by Jock Mahoney in <u>Rough, Tough West</u> (1952)

BIG & LITTLE

He's a small town big shot.
The Henchman was uncredited in <u>The Old Corral</u> (1936)

BITTERNESS

Swallow down your bitterness.
Elias Hobbes played by Wallace Ford in <u>The Great Jesse James Raid</u> (1953)

Bitterness can become a bad habit.
Dr. Enos Davis played by Cecil Kellaway in <u>The Proud Rebel</u> (1958)

BLESSINGS

Oh, it's wonderful! We got money and whiskey and lovely ladies; just had a beautiful fight. I tell ya, we really ought to be thankful for our blessings!
Randy McCall played by Lee Dixon in <u>Angel and the Badman</u> (1947)

May you long travel the path of life in days that are calm and peaceful.
Ruby Big Elk played by Dolores Brown in <u>Cimarron</u> (1931)

May the apple of your eye see only good. And may God make smooth the path before you.
Rock Mullaney played by David O'Hara in <u>Crossfire Trail</u> (2001)

Good luck. Green grass and running water.
Captain John C. Fremont played by Dana Andrews in <u>Kit Carson</u> (1940)

BLINDNESS

Blind men are so accommodating.
Chavez played by Patrick O'Neal in <u>El Condor</u> (1970)

None's so blind as they who will not see.
Grizzly Garth played by Tom Chatterton, paraphrasing Jonathan Swift and Matthew Henry, in <u>Home on the Range</u> (1946)

I was blind before. I couldn't see the hate in Emmett's heart.
Henry Westover played by Roy Scheider in <u>King of Texas</u> (2002)

Women close their eyes to a lot of things when they have their own man.
Cora Dean played by Jean Parker in <u>A Lawless Street</u> (1955)

A wink is as good as a nod to a blind horse.
Jake Harmon played by Robert Fiske in <u>Roaring Six Guns</u> (1937)

BLOOD

Riker: I ought to have a doctor! I've bled some!
Chisum: Not enough!
Karl Riker played by Gregg Palmer and John Chisum in <u>Chisum</u> (1970)

If we're going to let blood, we got to be prepared to smell it.
Reece Kilgore played by Lyle Bettger in <u>The Lone Ranger</u> (1956)

Chet: So I'm part Indian?
Otis: By blood you are. But blood only means what you let it.
Chet Payne played by Eddie Robinson and Otis Payne played by Ron Canada in <u>Lone Star</u> (1996)

Blood never lies.
Don Rafael Montero played by Stuart Wilson in <u>The Mask of Zorro</u> (1998)

Men ride longer over blood than money.
Gentry/John Coventry played by Fred MacMurray in <u>Quantez</u> (1957)

BLOOD BROTHER

The blood of each flows with the other. But they are still each other. The blood of many fathers is joined and will be passed on to many children. For blood is life and never dies. Each of you share it. And even when you are great distances apart, you will be together. You are joined as brothers.
The Indian Chief was uncredited in <u>Walk the Proud Land</u> (1956)

BLOOD POISONING

A guy can get blood poisoning from getting killed with a dirty bullet.
Milford Farnsworth played by Bob Hope in <u>Alias Jesse James</u> (1959)

BOASTING

Boast not thyself of tomorrow, son, for no man knows what the day may bring forth.
Bible Jude played by Richard Carlyle in <u>The Saddle Buster</u> (1932)

BODY & SOUL

A starved body has a skinny soul.
Emiliano Zapata played by Marlon Brando in <u>Viva Zapata!</u> (1952)

BOONE, DANIEL

Did you know that Daniel Boone was 84 years old when he crossed the Rockies?
Barbara Waggoman played by Cathy O'Donnell in <u>The Man from Laramie</u> (1955)

BOOT HILL

He's been cheatin' Boot Hill long enough.
Ed Slade played by John Merton in <u>The Lone Prairie</u> (1942)

There's a Boot Hill in every town where the dead are hidden in the ground and forgotten. There's a Boot Hill in every man's soul too.
Doc Weber played by John Carradine in <u>Showdown at Boot Hill</u> (1958)

BOOTS

They're like gloves but you wear them on your feet.
Margo Thomas played by Florence Rice in <u>The Kid from Texas</u> (1939)

BORROWING

I don't believe in borrowing ... not money or trouble.
Maggie Sergeant played by Joanna Pettet in <u>Pioneer Woman</u> (1973)

BOSS

Who died and left you in charge anyway?
Mandy played by Charlotte Ross in <u>Savage Land</u> (1994)

BOUNDARY

Passed into history are the days when the only boundaries in the West were the distant horizons.
Prologue in <u>Heart of the West</u> (1936)

BOYS & MEN

Don't send a boy to do a man's job.
Hort Moran played by Douglas Kennedy in <u>The Lone Gun</u> (1954)

When you watch someone grow up, you can't realize when he becomes a man.
Cole Younger played by Willard Parker in <u>Young Jesse James</u> (1960)

BRAINS

Use your head instead of your vocal cords!
Dr. Lee played by Frank Jaquet in <u>Call of the Rockies</u> (1944)

I'd knock his brains out if I knew where to hit him.
Big Boy Matson played by Woody Harrelson in <u>*The Hi-Lo Country*</u> *(1998)*

Your tongue and brain never have got acquainted with each other.
Mort Slade played by I. Stanford Jolley in <u>*The Kid Rides Again*</u> *(1943)*

Use your heads for something more than a place to keep your mouths.
Nugget Clark played by Eddy Waller in <u>*Vigilante Hideout*</u> *(1950)*

BRAVADO

Travis: The man sure is full of himself.
Bowie: Yeah, anybody who calls himself 'El Supremo' hasn't got much of a choice.
Col. William Barrett Travis played by Alec Baldwin and Jim Bowie played by James Arness in <u>*The Alamo: Thirteen Days to Glory*</u> *(1987)*

The snake that rattles or an enemy that shouts is not very dangerous.
McCord played by Bob Barron in <u>*Ballad of a Gunfighter*</u> *(1964)*

Big noise often stands on small legs.
Chief Mike played by Michael Granger in <u>*Battle of Rogue River*</u> *(1954)*

Your bark is a lot worse than your bite.
Billy the Kid played by Bob Steele in <u>*Billy the Kid in Texas*</u> *(1940)*

He is a snake without fangs.
Hawkeye played by Steve Forrest in <u>*Last of the Mohicans*</u> *(1977)*

BRAVERY

Sometimes it's easier to be brave than honest.
Sally played by Coleen Gray in <u>*Apache Drums*</u> *(1951)*

The trick to being brave is not to be too brave!
Captain Thomas Archer played by Richard Widmark in <u>*Cheyenne Autumn*</u> *(1964)*

You don't look for bravery in a lady.
Captain Thomas Thompson played by Ben Johnson in <u>Fort Bowie</u> (1958)

I ain't got any hankering to be the bravest man in the cemetery!
Sheriff of Kirk County played by Hal Price in <u>Oklahoma Annie</u> (1952)

BREAKS

I always give a game guy a break. I plugged him in the back so he wouldn't see it coming.
Denver Jones played by Don Porter in <u>Cripple Creek</u> (1952)

BRIDGES

Let's not cross our bridges until we come to them.
Doug Ransom played by George Eldredge in <u>The Lone Star Trail</u> (1943)

BROKEN HEARTS

The heart is like one of those old Chinese vases. It has enough cracks in it to look like a spider web, but it'll still hold together.
Belle Devalle played by Gypsy Rose Lee in <u>Belle of the Yukon</u> (1944)

There's nothing like whiskey for a broken heart.
Jess Griswold played by Rod Cameron in <u>Santa Fe Passage</u> (1955)

BRONC RIDING

It's just like dancing with a girl, only you let him lead.
Jeff McCloud played by Robert Mitchum in <u>The Lusty Men</u> (1952)

BUFFALO BILL

Bill Cody was a good man. But he wasn't half as good as his publicity.
Wyatt Earp played by James Garner in <u>Sunset</u> (1988)

BULL RIDERS

He don't want me on his back. He wants me on the ground where he can dance on me. He's wild and free, just a part of nature. And sometimes, when the chute opens and they turn us loose, just sometimes, something magic happens and I'm part of that animal. For eight seconds I get to be wild and free and uncontrolled. And when I make that ride, and then I hit the ground and raise my hands, and everyone yells, it is worth it!

H.D. Dalton played by Scott Glenn in <u>My Heroes Have Always Been Cowboys</u> (1992)

BULLETS

There's no love in a bullet.

Wilson played by Robert Mitchum in <u>Bandido</u> (1956)

Bullets are liable to hit promiscuous-like so you better stay inside.

Sheriff Masters played by Ted Adams in <u>Billy the Kid Trapped</u> (1942)

None of us is bulletproof.

Sheriff Gifford played by Hugh Sanders in <u>City of Bad Men</u> (1953)

A bullet hole makes a man powerful thirsty.

Sheriff Matt Verity played by Al Bridge in <u>Cowboy Counsellor</u> (1932)

If a stray bullet comes this way, it ain't fussy as to whose head it bumps into.

Luke played by Charles Irwin in <u>The Sheriff of Fractured Jaw</u> (1958)

BULLS

You're always charging around like a bull in a china shop.

J. Richard Bentley played by Douglas Fowley in <u>Along the Navajo Trail</u> (1945)

There are only two ways you can ride a bull. You can either make it happen or you can let it happen.

Hank Braxton played by Kiefer Sutherland in <u>Cowboy Up</u> (2001)

If you get born a bull, you got a ninety percent chance of getting castrated and served up as hamburgers. So, on balance, I reckon I'd choose being a cow.
Tom Booker played by Robert Redford in The Horse Whisperer *(1998)*

I think there must be a bull in the life of every one of us. And someday when it comes rushing at us, there is the question: do we have courage or do we run away?
Pepe Ortiz as himself in The Littlest Outlaw *(1955)*

BULLY

I hate bullies because a bully doesn't just beat you up. He takes away your dignity.
Phil Berquist played by Daniel Stern in City Slickers *(1991)*

BURIALS

Please do not try to bury me before I'm dead.
Leslie Edwards played by Matthew Perry in Almost Heroes *(1998)*

It's the best I could bury you, Danny. I'm sorry.
(Last farewell to brother as the body is thrown from a moving train in a mail sack, off a train trestle, into the river below.) Jim Larsen played by Fred MacMurray in Face of a Fugitive *(1959)*

Even the devil deserves a proper burial.
Narration by Noel Hickman, played by Chuck Pierce, Jr., in Hawken's Breed *(1987)*

Laughton: There's room in the churchyard. You can bury him there.
Taggart: Thanks, Sheriff, but Slocum never did get along with strangers.
Sheriff Laughton played by Ernest Borgnine and O.B. Taggart played by Mickey Rooney in Outlaws: The Legend of O.B. Taggart *(1994)*

Lola: Tell me about my dear, dear daddy. Is it true that he's dead?
Stanley: Well, we hope he is. They buried him.
Lola Marcel played by Sharon Lynn and Stanley played by Stan Laurel in Way Out West *(1937)*

BUSINESS

Never keep a customer waiting and never let one get away.
Dobson played by George Lloyd in <u>Bandit King of Texas</u> (1949)

Ethan: A man of value never places his business above friendship.
Brady: This was a friendship based on business.
Ethan played by Rich Rossovich and Brady Hawkes played by Kenny Rogers in <u>The Gambler Returns: The Luck of the Draw</u> (1991)

I don't let sentiment interfere with business.
Matilda Boggs played by Patricia Knox in <u>Gentlemen with Guns</u> (1946)

You'll learn that it pays to be agreeable.
Mort Slade played by I. Stanford Jolley in <u>The Kid Rides Again</u> (1943)

This is a business. If we don't run it like a business, we're going to be out of business.
Vern Kidston played by Keith Carradine in <u>Last Stand at Saber River</u> (1997)

Grown men know that business sometimes gets dirty. But the dirtier the business, the more cleanly it has to be handled.
James Landry played by Jeffrey Nordling in <u>The Lone Ranger</u> (2003)

In our business, a little dishonesty is necessary now and then.
James Barlow played by Randolph Scott in <u>Rage at Dawn</u> (1955)

Bradford: Why don't you stay where people are? That's good business.
Fargo: Go where people are going. That's better business.
Bradford played by Granville Bates and William Fargo played by Jack Clark in <u>Wells Fargo</u> (1937)

There's nothing like looking prosperous when you set out to make a business deal.
Pop Melbern played by Jason Robards, Sr., in <u>Wild Horse Mesa</u> (1947)

CANNIBALISM

It's lonely being a cannibal; tough making friends.
Colonel Hart played by Jeffrey Jones in Ravenous (1999)

CATHOLICS

Brisco: Where did you learn how to throw a punch like that?
Amanda: Catholic school.
Brisco County, Jr., played by Bruce Campbell and Amanda played by Anne Tremko in Adventures of Brisco County, Jr. (1993)

Alacran: Out of respect for God, I will spare the church. But the town is going to burn.
Priest: You are worse than the soldiers!
Alacran: That is true. But at least we're good Catholics!

Alacran played by Robert Davi and Father Malone played by Ian McElhinney in Blind Justice (1994)

CATS

Chris: It seems to me you're a great deal more cat than kitten.
Estelle: Let's just say I've come of age.
Chris Foster played by Audie Murphy and Estelle played by Kathleen Crowley in Showdown (1963)

CATS & DOGS

I just want a cat that is more like a dog.
Miss Kitty's voice by Amy Irving in An American Tail: Fievel Goes West *(1991)*

CAUSES

There is no difference between a lost cause and a lost dog. They both taste the same.
The Hotel Manager played by Manuel Sanchez Navarro in Bandido *(1956)*

Lorn: Do you believe in fighting for lost causes even when you know they're lost?
Jeannie: If they're right, yes.
Lorn Crawford played by Hugh Marlowe and Jeannie played by Coleen Gray in The Black Whip *(1956)*

Your cause is just. But if you take food from the jaguar's mouth, he will try to kill you.
Ramon played by José Manuel Martin in Five Giants from Texas *(1966)*

There's nothing like a good cause to keep you going.
Davis Healy played by Bruce Boxleitner in Gunsmoke: One Man's Justice *(1994)*

It makes no sense to die for a lost cause.
Rev. Alden played by Dabbs Greer in Little House: The Last Farewell *(1984)*

CAUTION

I'm not the kind of guy that does things suddenly. I got to look before I leap.
Quirt Evans played by John Wayne in Angel and the Badman *(1947)*

It's better to be safe than sorry.
Hendricks played by Harry Woods in Blue Mountain Skies *(1939)*

Caution makes for a longer life.
Bill Miner/George Edwards played by Richard Farnsworth in The Grey Fox *(1982)*

Keep your nose in the wind and your eyes along the skyline.
Del Gue played by Stefan Gierasch in <u>Jeremiah Johnson</u> (1972)

You got to learn not to run headlong into things.
Gentry/John Coventry played by Fred MacMurray in <u>Quantez</u> (1957)

I only take one step at a time. That's why I was given two feet.
La Boeuf played by Glen Campbell in <u>True Grit</u> (1969)

CHAIN

I've never yet seen a rusty chain that didn't have a weak link in it somewhere.
Wild Bill Hickok played by Bill Elliott in <u>King of Dodge City</u> (1941)

CHALLENGE

You don't help men like Corrigan. You challenge them. Then they succeed.
Beauvais played by Dan Duryea in <u>River Lady</u> (1948)

CHAMPION

If you want to be a champion, it's a lonely road.
J.R. Patterson played by Candy Clark in <u>Rodeo Girl</u> (1980)

CHANCES

You don't get wealthy if you don't take chances.
Abby Nixon played by Virginia Mayo in <u>Devil's Canyon</u> (1953)

Sometimes it's good to learn when not to take a chance.
Will Keough played by Fred MacMurray in <u>Gun for a Coward</u> (1957)

I know that if you want to win, you got to take a chance. You got to add something to the pot.
John Wesley Hardin played by Rock Hudson in <u>The Lawless Breed</u> (1952)

CHANGE

The desire to change must come from within.
Madeline Hammond played by Jo Ann Sayers in <u>The Light of Western Stars</u> *(1940)*

Judy: You can't change what's past.
Jet: But we can change the future.
Judy Polsen played by Joan Evans and Jet Cosgrave played by John Derek in <u>The Outcast</u> *(1954)*

Folks can outgrow most anything if they try.
Hopalong Cassidy played by William Boyd in <u>Partners of the Plains</u> *(1938)*

Jill: When you're young, you always believe that things are going to change for the better.
Luke: Well, what do you believe?
Jill: They change all right, mostly for the worse.
Jill Crane played by Carole Mathews and Luke Welsh played by Charles Bronson in <u>Showdown at Boot Hill</u> *(1958)*

After water has been frozen for twenty years, you can't thaw it out with a sudden warm spell.
Amanda Griffith played by Helen Broderick in <u>Stand Up and Fight</u> *(1939)*

Bob: Maybe I've changed.
Betty: A coyote never changes his bark.
Bob Russell played by Wheeler Oakman and Betty Owen played by Alice Day in <u>Two Fisted Law</u> *(1932)*

It is good for people to change but not forget.
Blue Elk played by John War Eagle in <u>When the Legends Die</u> *(1972)*

CHAOS

You know, Nietzsche says, out of chaos comes order.
Howard Johnson played by John Hillerman in <u>Blazing Saddles</u> (1974)

CHARACTER

People don't get their character from their names.
Hannah Brockway played by Evelyn Keyes in <u>Renegades</u> (1946)

Georgia: He [father] lets me have anything I want.
Euphemia: But that makes for poor character.
*Young Georgia Lawshe played by Rachael Leigh Cook and Young Euphemia Ashby
played by Tina Majorino in <u>True Women</u> (1997)*

CHARITY

I've never seen it fail. Give a man charity and they break the hand that feeds them.
Cyrus Higbee played by Don Beddoe in <u>Blue Canadian Rockies</u> (1952)

He who accepts charity with good grace makes happy the giver.
Priscilla Lock played by Cecil Cunningham in <u>Cowboy Serenade</u> (1942)

Charity always helps those who give it.
Daniel Wheeler played by Lance Henriksen in <u>Into the West</u> (2005)

I thought it was one of those charity affairs where they let you in for nothing
and then charge you to get out.
Jason Sweet played by Glenn Ford in <u>The Sheepman</u> (1958)

CHARLATANS

The prime requisite of charlatans is their ability to fake sincerity.
Bruce Barkow played by Mark Harmon in <u>Crossfire Trail</u> (2001)

CHASE

I'm saying we're chasing a bad guess only.
Joshua Everette played by James Whitmore in Chato's Land (1972)

They went thataway!
Fuzzy played by Fuzzy Knight in The Cowboy and the Señorita (1944)

Hoke: How far do you think she'll chase us?
Dingus: You stole her money and her heart, and you burned down her whorehouse. How far do you think?
Herkimer "Hoke" Birdsill played by George Kennedy and Dingus Magee played by Frank Sinatra in Dirty Dingus Magee (1970)

Nobody can chase you if you don't run.
Zach Provo played by James Coburn in The Last Hard Men (1976)

I got a piece of your shadow and I ain't never gonna let go.
Calamity Jane played by Abby Dalton in The Plainsman (1966)

Johnny: They're gone!
Doc: They're gone. Well, goddamn Dobbs, that's a right smart observation. When folks ain't where they used to be, they're normally gone!
Johnny Dobbs played by R.L. Tolbert and Doc Shabitt played by Matt Clark in The Quick and the Dead (1987)

Out to get and getting is two different things.
Bill Boone played by Bill Elliott in The Return of Daniel Boone (1941)

CHEEKS

Captain: What happened to turning the other cheek, Padre?
Priest: I grew tired of bloody cheeks.
Federal Captain played by Jordi Molla and the Priest played by Joaquim de Almeida in Dollar for the Dead (1998)

CHEERFULNESS

Sgt.: But how do you force the people to be cheerful against their will?

Capitan: That is your responsibility, Sergeant. But I want them cheerful even if you have to shoot them!

Sgt. Garcia played by Henry Calvin and Capitan Monastario played by Britt Lomond in The Sign of Zorro (1960)

CHIEFS

In an Indian teepee, you will learn the woman is always chief.

White Bull played by Sal Mineo in Tonka (1958)

CHILDREN

It's kind of a shame kids have to grow up into people.

Davy Crockett played by John Wayne in The Alamo (1960)

Lorry: When are you going to stop treating me like a child?

Gabby: When you stop acting like one.

Lorry Alastair played by Dale Evans and Gabby Whittaker played by George "Gabby" Hayes in Along the Navajo Trail (1945)

I can't think of anything tougher than burying one of your own children.

Bill Huntoon played by Wilford Brimley in The Boys of Twilight: The Road Back (1992)

It's hard to believe that one child can bring so much happiness, so much grief.

The Padre played by Andrew Duggan in The Bravados (1958)

We can't live our children's lives for them.

Yancey Cravat played by Richard Dix in Cimarron (1931)

Children should never have to see the things we do.

Don Rafael Montero played by Stuart Wilson in The Mask of Zorro (1998)

CHOICES

When you're faced with a choice, go after the best of both.
Banjo Hackett played by Don Meredith in <u>Banjo Hackett: Roamin' Free</u> *(1976)*

Hatch: A man can't choose who he is.
Woodruff: Well, he can damn well choose how he conducts himself.
Hatch played by Haig Sutherland and Sgt. Woodruff played by William MacDonald in <u>The Colt</u> *(2005)*

People have to make choices. And choices never are perfect.
Babson played by John Litel in <u>The Kentuckian</u> *(1955)*

Sometimes one must cut off the finger to save a hand.
Master Po played by Keye Luke in <u>Kung Fu</u> *(1972)*

A few bad choices and a man can lose his soul.
Doc Woods/Doc Holliday played by Randy Quaid in <u>Purgatory</u> *(1999)*

Do you know what makes life hard, Brady? The fact that it always forces us into making a choice. And if we do not make the choice, it is always made for us.
Governor Cipriano Castro played by Pedro Armendaris in <u>The Wonderful Country</u> *(1959)*

CHRISTMAS

All I want for Christmas is to be surrounded by the people we care about.
Missie played by Erin Cottrell in <u>Love's Long Journey</u> *(2005)*

Christmas is just another working day.
Ike Franklin played by David Carradine in <u>Miracle at Sage Creek</u> *(2005)*

Barlett: I wonder what a peaceful, harmonious Christmas would be like?
Sarah: Boring!
Barlett McClure played by Powers Boothe and Sarah McClure played by Dana Delany in <u>True Women</u> *(1997)*

CHURCH

There's something peaceful about a church bell.
Kate Hardison played by Marguerite Chapman in <u>Coroner Creek</u> (1948)

A little country church is as wonderful as a great cathedral because it stands for the same things.
Susan Crowell played by Dorinda Clifton in <u>King of the Range</u> (1947)

Now you're trying to build a church, and I don't think you want a hanging tree alongside of it.
Reverend Samuel Woods played by Van Heflin in <u>The Outcasts of Poker Flat</u> (1937)

Any community can do without a church. But think how much more a community can be with one, especially for those who want it, let alone those who need it.
Eddie Dean played himself in <u>Romance of the West</u> (1946)

A church picnic is like the Kingdom of Heaven. Everybody's welcome but you got to qualify.
Preacher Sam Shelby played by Chill Wills in <u>Young Guns of Texas</u> (1962)

CIGARS

There's something more friendly about a cigar from a friend, especially if it's a good cigar.
Colonel Davis played by Howard C. Hickman in <u>Robin Hood of the Pecos</u> (1941)

When I pass on to glory, my one wish will be to go with a pocketful of cigars. Where I'm going, there'll be no problem lighting them.
Jim Flood played by Barry Sullivan in <u>Seven Ways from Sundown</u> (1960)

CIVIL WAR

I know what I went home to: a rock chimney and a pile of ashes.
Clint played by Audie Murphy in <u>Arizona Raiders</u> (1965)

You feel South and North depending on what's in your heart.
Doc Grunch played by George "Gabby" Hayes in <u>Dark Command</u> *(1940)*

I never thought I'd live to see the day that a president of the United States would raise an army to invade his own country.
General Robert E. Lee played by Robert Duvall in <u>Gods and Generals</u> *(2003)*

Boston: If there's a war, I'm North, a Yankee. You're South. What happens to us?
Owen: I shoot you, I guess.
Boston Grant played by Ruth Roman and Owen Pentecost played by Robert Stack in <u>Great Day in the Morning</u> *(1956)*

That war was a widow-maker.
The Narrator was Robert Sampson in <u>Pharaoh's Army</u> *(1995)*

CIVILIZATION

The coming of too many people always brings law and order, churches, schools, and a lot of crackpots against gambling and drinking.
Joe Morino played by Dennis Moore in <u>Driftin' River</u> *(1946)*

It takes more than rifles to make a new civilization. It takes spinning wheels too.
Alice Munro played by Binnie Barnes in <u>The Last of the Mohicans</u> *(1936)*

You can't give an Indian a plow and a horse and a piece of land, and expect him to be civilized.
The Townsman was uncredited in <u>The Oklahoman</u> *(1957)*

There's only one solution: exterminate them; burn out their villages. That's the only way to bring civilization to these parts.
Captain Arnold Vaugant played by Richard Rober in <u>The Savage</u> *(1952)*

CLEANLINESS

A new broom sweeps clean.
Molly Morgan played by Marjorie Reynolds in <u>Six-Shootin' Sheriff</u> *(1938)*

CLOTHES

It takes more than clothes to make a man.
Colonel Lambeth played by Thurston Hall in <u>West of the Pecos</u> *(1945)*

CO-EXISTENCE

The West is getting smaller, friends, and I reckon we got to learn to live together.
Reece Duncan played by Alexander Scourby in <u>The Redhead from Wyoming</u> *(1953)*

COAXING

Sometimes a mule can be coaxed when he can't be driven.
Lilli Marsh played by Evelyn Brent in <u>Hopalong Cassidy Returns</u> *(1936)*

CODE OF THE WEST

I'm not armed. There's a law of the West: no one shoots an unarmed man.
Reflections by John Tunstall, played by Andrew Bicknell (just prior to being gunned down), in <u>Gore Vidal's Billy the Kid</u> *(1989)*

COFFEE

I like my coffee strong enough to float a pistol.
Shep Horgan played by Ernest Borgnine in <u>Jubal</u> *(1956)*

You know, this coffee is just like you. You think it's one thing, then you find out it's something else again.
Sam Cooper played by Van Heflin in <u>The Ruthless Four</u> *(1968)*

COLD

He used to complain about the cold. So one day I decided to do that boy a favor, and I made him a nice overcoat out of wood. It cured him of sneezing.
Sheriff Gideon Burnett played by Frank Wolff in <u>The Great Silence</u> *(1969)*

COMFORT

Like the man said, all a fella needs is a cup of coffee and a good smoke.
Old Tom played by John Carradine in <u>Johnny Guitar</u> (1954)

Just as snug as a bug in a rug.
Breezy played by Jack Luden in <u>Phantom Gold</u> (1938)

When you live together for a dozen years, you realize that comfort is not what counts.
Charlie Anderson played by James Stewart in <u>Shenandoah</u> (1965)

Cheryl: I just need to be held.
Wyatt: At one time or another we all do.
Cheryl King played by Mariel Hemingway and Wyatt Earp played by James Garner in <u>Sunset</u> (1988)

COMMITMENT

Plans, promises, dreams: they're easy to make but hard to keep.
Blaine Madden played by Rory Calhoun in <u>The Gun Hawk</u> (1963)

COMMON GOOD

Sometimes the common good can run over people like a freight train.
Payton McCay played by Bruce Dern in <u>Deadman's Revenge</u> (1994)

COMMON GROUND

We got to find some common meeting ground to settle our differences.
Charles Alderson played by William "Wild Bill" Elliott in <u>Wyoming</u> (1947)

COMMUNICATION

John: You don't listen!
Rupert: I listen perfectly well!
John: Well, then, you don't hear!
John Thornton played by Rick Schroder and Rupert played by Vince Metcalfe in <u>Call of the Wild</u> (1992)

President: I take it you disagree with what's being said here, sir.

Sam: Rather with what's not being said, Mr. President.

President Chester A. Arthur played by Larry Gates and Sam Brassfield played by Robert Taylor in <u>Cattle King</u> (1963)

Your voice, it don't match the words you say.

The Cisco Kid played by Cesar Romero in <u>The Cisco Kid and the Lady</u> (1939)

There's some things that are better said than written.

Matt Telford played by Donald Randolph in <u>Gunsmoke</u> (1953)

You can't tell somebody something if they don't stop talking long enough for you to tell them what you want to tell them.

Charles Ingalls played by Michael Landon in <u>Little House: The Last Farewell</u> (1984)

You can't talk to a woman who doesn't understand what you're talking about.

Buck Wyatt played by Robert Taylor in <u>Westward the Women</u> (1952)

His lips are saying one thing while his eyes are saying something else.

Janey Nolan played by Betty Brewer in <u>Wild Bill Hickok Rides</u> (1942)

COMMNICATION & INDIANS

You have made the crooked tongue speak straight.

Chief Mike played by Michael Granger in <u>Battle of Rogue River</u> (1954)

Buffalo Horn: This is the way for men to talk. Their eyes see if words are true or false.

Pacer: You talk. I will listen.

Buffalo Horn played by Rodolfo Acosta and Pacer Burton played by Elvis Presley in <u>Flaming Star</u> (1960)

The white eyes speak with the tongue of the crow, noise which means nothing.

Dark Thunder played by Pat Hogan in <u>Overland Pacific</u> (1954)

The white man speaks with many tongues, all of them twisted.
Sitting Bull played by J. Carrol Naish in Sitting Bull (1954)

COMMUNITY

You can't build a strong community out of weak people.
Wade Proctor played by Grant Withers in The Savage Horde (1950)

COMPANY

Wild Bill: I see you're still not careful of the company you keep.
Mitch: That's right. Otherwise, what would I be doing standing here talking to you?
Wild Bill Hickok played by William "Wild Bill" Elliott and Mitch Carew played by Dick Curtis in Across the Sierras (1941)

Don't ever be alone with yourself, Blaine. You wouldn't like it.
Duke Winston played by Addison Richards in Back in the Saddle (1941)

Walking around with a pistol in your hand isn't exactly the best way to get along with me.
Doc Lowen played by Leonardo Pieraccioni in Gunslinger's Revenge (2005)

Birdie: A woman doesn't hold a candle to a man for company, do you think?
Dan: Well, that depends on your point of view.
Birdie played by Barbara Nichols and Dan Kehoe played by Clark Gable in The King and Four Queens (1956)

If you can't get along with each other, you can get along without each other.
Otis Ellis played by Paul Hurst in Law of the Golden West (1949)

Jim: Do you mind if I ride along with ya?
Big Davey: It ain't my forest.
Jim Fairways played by Robert Mitchum and David "Big Davey" Harvey played by William Holden in Rachel and the Stranger (1948)

I believe I'd truly enjoy seeing your face on a milk carton.
Marshal Del Wilkes played by John Enos in <u>Raven Hawk</u> (1996)

It doesn't matter where you are; it's whom you're with.
Bob Merritt played by Robert Lowery in <u>Shooting High</u> (1940)

You're harder to get rid of than the seven-year itch!
Lucky Jenkins played by Russell Hayden in <u>Silver on the Sage</u> (1939)

Two's company and three's a crowd.
Buck Weylan played by Buck Jones in <u>The Stranger from Arizona</u> (1938)

COMPASSION

There's no sense kicking a man when he's down.
Hopalong Cassidy played by William Boyd in <u>Partners of the Plains</u> (1938)

COMPATIBILITY

You know the old saying: difficult to live with, impossible to live without.
General Frederick McCabe played by Andrew Duggan in <u>The Glory Guys</u> (1965)

The worst thing that could happen to either of them is for them to end up together.
Carl Miller played by Rod Cameron in <u>San Antone</u> (1953)

COMPETITION

Competition is the spice of life.
Honest John Travers played by Cy Kendall in <u>Outlaw Trail</u> (1944)

COMPLAINING

If Jewell lived in a castle, she'd complain it was the wrong color.
Rip Metcalf played by Kris Kristofferson in <u>Pair of Aces</u> (1990)

COMPLIMENTS

I don't like back-handed compliments.

Idaho Jones played by Harold Goodman in <u>The Scarlet Horseman</u> (1946)

CONCEALMENT

The wise man who wishes to hide covers his face with the mask of night.

Don Arturo Bordega played by Cornel Wilde in <u>California Conquest</u> (1952)

CONCEIT

You're so conceited that if you fell in love with anybody else it would be a triangle.

Charlie Davenport played by Keenan Wynn in <u>Annie Get Your Gun</u> (1950)

CONDITIONING

Well, now don't you worry. From here on out, I'll take over your training. And one month from now, you'll either be in top shape or two weeks dead.

Artemus Gordon played by Ross Martin in <u>The Wild Wild West Revisited</u> (1979)

CONFESSION

Them that say confession is good for your soul is overlooking the load it takes off the chest.

Nugget Clark played by Eddy Waller in <u>Bandit King of Texas</u> (1949)

Mister, I've tried everything except confession. Even God wouldn't believe that!

The Saloon Girl was uncredited in <u>Bite the Bullet</u> (1975)

CONFIDENCE GAME

All confidence games are aimed at people who want something for nothing.

Candy Johnson played by Clark Gable in <u>Honky Tonk</u> (1941)

CONFLICT RESOLUTION

At the very first time there's a problem, it's goodbye principle and pass the ammunition.

Amy Kane played by Suzanna Thompson in <u>High Noon</u> (2000)

You don't settle Indian troubles by shooting Sitting Bull's son in the back.
Robert Parrish played by Dale Robertson in Sitting Bull (1954)

CONGRESS

Being in Congress has ruined many a good man.
The Gambler played by Denver Pyle in The Alamo (1960)

The thing about my little jokes is, take 'em or leave 'em, they don't hurt anybody. But with Congress, every time they make a joke, it's a law. And every time they make a law, it's a joke.
Will Rogers played by Will Rogers, Jr., in The Story of Will Rogers (1952)

CONSCIENCE

I don't have to live with people, but I do have to live with my conscience.
Lt. Frank Hewitt played by Audie Murphy in The Guns of Fort Petticoat (1957)

How much is it worth to have a clear conscience?
The Preacher played by Clint Eastwood in Pale Rider (1985)

Once you learn to toss your conscience out of the window, nothing matters.
Jeff Travis played by Randolph Scott in The Stranger Wore a Gun (1953)

CONSCIENTIOUS OBJECTOR

Nora: Mr. Farraday is a conscientious objector.
Farraday: Not conscientious, just objecting.
Nora Curtis played by Joanne Dru and James Farraday played by Van Johnson in Siege at Red River (1954)

CONTEMPT OF COURT

If it's a crime to show contempt for this court, then I'm a criminal.
Duke Lassiter played by Albert Dekker in Wyoming (1947)

CONTRACT

A man's contract just doesn't get handed down to his relatives like his old clothes.
Chantry played by Olin Howlin in Stage to Tucson (1950)

CONTRITION

And I take back every nasty thing I ever said about you, practically.
Toni Ames played by Dale Evans in Don't Fence Me In (1945)

CONVENT

Teresa: I was asking the Holy Mother to save me from the convent. Is that a sin?
Zorro [posing as Padre]: Oh, the sin, I think, would be in sending you to one.
Teresa played by Anne Archer and Don Diego/Zorro played by Frank Langella in The Mark of Zorro (1974)

CONVERSATION

Judy: You make conversation very difficult.
Jed: You make it unnecessary.
Judy Parker played by Lynne Roberts and Jed Kilton played by Richard Arlen in The Big Bonanza (1944)

COOKS

Buckshot: How much am I going to get paid for cooking?
Winky: You'll be paid what you're worth.
Buckshot: Well, you better get a new cook because I don't work that cheap!
Buckshot Peters played by Wally Vernon and Winky Gordon played by Twinkle Watts in Outlaws of Santa Fe (1944)

Gabe: Do you cook anything besides beans?
Eagle Eye: More beans.
Gabe McBride played by Robert Conrad and Eagle Eye played by Byron Chief Moon in Samurai Cowboy (1993)

Ginger: I'll learn to cook if it kills me.
Chito: All I hope is it doesn't kill me!
Ginger Kelly played by Virginia Owen and Chito Rafferty played by Richard Martin in Thunder Mountain (1947)

CORPORAL PUNISHMENT
You don't find justice at the end of a rope.
Jim Lassiter played by George Montgomery in Riders of the Purple Sage (1941)

CORPSES
Some of my best friends are corpses. They're the only ones you can trust. Oh sure, they stink a little. But no more then a few live ones I know.
The Con Man played by Edward G. Robinson in The Outrage (1964)

He's pretty healthy-looking for a corpse.
Stan Borden played by Milburn Stone in The Phantom Cowboy (1941)

He was such a handsome man. He'll make such a magnificent corpse.
Duchess played by Ruth Donnelly in The Spoilers (1955)

CORPUS DELICTI
Corpus delicti. That's Latin for 'go get the coffin.'
The Sheriff played by Smiley Burnette in South of Death Valley (1949)

COSTS
It is much when one has nothing.
Juan Vazcaro played by George J. Lewis in The Big Sombrero (1949)

You get what you pay for and pay for what you get.
Connie Lane played by Edith Fellows in Heart of the Rio Grande (1942)

You just don't get things for nothing.
Jen Larrabee played by Gail Davis in On Top of Old Smoky (1953)

One way or the other, you pay for everything you get.
Hemp Brown played by Rory Calhoun in The Saga of Hemp Brown (1958)

Our mission is to capture these men at all costs. But I want the cost to be on their side.
Leander McNelly played by Dylan McDermott in Texas Rangers (2001)

COUNTRY

I guess the country lasts forever and people ain't but for a little while.
John Grady Cole played by Matt Damon in All the Pretty Horses (2000)

You forget it took the little man as well as the big one to make this country what it is.
Dan Taylor played by Richard Dix in American Empire (1942)

This is a country in transition, filled with beauty and despair.
Kate Flynn played by Jackie Burroughs in The Grey Fox (1982)

Andy: What do you think of our beautiful western country?
Jackson: All right, I guess, but I can't see it. The trees and the hills is in the way.
Andy McBride played by Robert Paige and Jackson played by Willie Best in The Red Stallion (1947)

If God had wanted to give the world an enema, He'd have stuck the needle in here.
Emmet played by Ken Hutchinson in The Wrath of God (1972)

COUP STICK

To strike an enemy with a coup stick and leave him humiliated but unarmed was a war honor of the highest rank.
Grandpa/Old Pete Chasing Horse played by August Schellenberg in Dreamkeeper (2003)

COUPLES

I always say, the longer they don't get married, the happier the couple will be.
Squint played by Paul E. Burns in Fury at Gunsight Pass (1956)

Two souls without a single thought.
DeLuxe Harry played by Harry Gripp in <u>The Great K&A Robbery</u> (1926)

COURAGE

Courage is a powerful thing but it ain't something a man loses. It just gets misplaced sometimes.
The Stranger played by Martin Sheen in <u>Ballad of a Gunfighter</u> (1999)

Never argue with a man's courage.
Colonel Jonathan Bixby played by Henry Hull in <u>The Return of the Cisco Kid</u> (1939)

Preacher: You have no faith, sister!
Ada: You have no balls, preacher!
The Preacher played by Bruce E. Murrow and Ada played by Sandra Ellis Lafferty in <u>Steel Frontier</u> (1995)

What happens isn't important. What is important is the courage with which you meet it. Anybody can cheer when he wins. But when he loses, it takes a big man to pick up the pieces and start all over.
Rob McLaughlin played by Preston Foster in <u>Thunderhead—Son of Flicka</u> (1945)

COURTSHIP

I guess it's pretty hard for a gal to play hard to get when she wants to be got.
Alkali played by William Fawcett in <u>Cattle Queen</u> (1951)

Now you see, Jack, that's the way it is with men and women. Lots of times men make some promises, then take their pleasures, and move on. Now on the other side of the ledger, you ought to understand that when a woman finally surrenders to a man, she's usually got him just about where she wants him.
Calamity Jane played by Ellen Barkin in <u>Wild Bill</u> (1995)

COWARD

Mortality, the last bastion of a coward.
Colonel Ives/Colqhoun played by Robert Carlyle in Ravenous (1999)

COWBOYS

I've chased down many a man in my day. But the plain fact is, cowboys are easy to rope but hard to ride.
Kate Muldoon played by Linda Evans in The Gambler Returns: The Luck of the Draw (1991)

Nobody gets to be a cowboy forever.
Chet Rollins played by Keith Carradine in Monte Walsh (2003)

Chet: You ever been in love, Monte?
Monte: No, I've been a cowboy all my life.
Chet Rollins played by Keith Carradine and Monte Walsh played by Tom Selleck in Monte Walsh (2003)

Cowboys don't get married unless they stop being cowboys.
Monte Walsh played by Tom Selleck in Monte Walsh (2003)

I just don't feel right in kissing a girl without my boots on.
Waco/Bert Ford played by Lee Bennett in Stars Over Texas (1946)

Isn't this great! I mean, here we are, cowboys singing around a campfire and eating beans!
Dean Ellis played by David Andrews in Wild Horses (1985)

COYOTE

The coyote speaks from the protection of the pack.
Jim Aherne/War Bonnet played by Charlton Heston in The Savage (1952)

CREDENTIALS

You don't come with the best recommendations: a temper and the son of a dead gunslinger.

Honest John Barrett played by Robert Middleton in <u>The Proud Ones</u> *(1956)*

CRIPPLES

In each of us there lives a crippled child.

Sgt. John Chawk, reading passage from journal, played by Van Heflin in <u>They Came to Cordura</u> *(1959)*

CROSS

We want you to know that the farmers all over the state are uniting to battle the big eastern trusts. So you just remember William Jennings Bryan's speech: 'Man will not be crucified on a cross of gold.'

Senator Willard Endicott played by Gary Swanson in <u>Blood Red</u> *(1988)*

CROWD

I never figured a crowd to be nice, just big.

Doc Adams played by Douglas Fowley in <u>Man from Del Rio</u> *(1956)*

CUSTER, GEORGE ARMSTRONG

You're the only man I know who reached the top of his profession, and was on his way down before he was thirty.

General Philip Sheridan played by Lawrence Tierney in <u>Custer of the West</u> *(1968)*

Gold was not the treasure Custer sought. But gold brought him something just as precious: his chance to focus attention on himself and shine as bright as any golden nugget in the public eye.

Narration in <u>The Great Sioux Massacre</u> *(1965)*

CUTTING

When you cut, use a sharp knife and do it quickly.

Calla Gaxton played by Dorothy Malone in <u>Pillars of the Sky</u> *(1956)*

DANCING

I'd just as soon not do my dancing at the end of a rope.
California Carlson played by Andy Clyde in <u>Border Patrol</u> (1943)

Captain: The lady and I were trying to dance.
Alejandro: You were trying. She was succeeding.
Captain Harrison Love played by Matt Letscher and Alejandro Murrieta played by Antonio Banderas in <u>The Mask of Zorro</u> (1998)

DANGER

There's nothing like a common danger to weld people together.
Martin Treadwell played by Will Wright in <u>Brimstone</u> (1949)

A man can't keep out of danger by hiding under the bed.
Michael Fabian played by Barry Fitzgerald in <u>California</u> (1946)

DARE

In my country we have a saying: one who does not dare does not live.
Rondo played by John Saxton in <u>The Plunderers</u> (1960)

DARKNESS

Darkness is a great equalizer for a blind man.
Ralph Hamilton played by Don Haggerty in Cattle Empire (1958)

In the end, there's only the darkness. It reigns the glorious color of all banners. And in the dust, all battle flags are gray.
Cortina played by Joaquim de Almeida in One Man's Hero (1999)

The powers of darkness sometimes do prevail.
Dr. Lucas Henry played by David Carradine in The Outsider (2002)

DATING

A date in a graveyard makes a guy wonder.
Jimmy Ryan played by Guy Madison in The Beast of Hollow Mountain (1956)

DAUGHTERS

Having a daughter is a real trial. A man with a son can get all the sleep he needs. But with a daughter, you can't close your eyes until everyone has gone home.
Uncle Willie McLeod played by Edgar Buchanan in The Desperadoes (1943)

DEAD OR ALIVE

Brady: Can you take 'em back alive?
Pinkerton Agent: That is my intention, but it is their choice.
Brady Hawkes played by Kenny Rogers and Pinkerton Agent Frank Dimaio played by Richard Riehle in Gambler V: Playing for Keeps (1994)

DEALS

I know it's a crappy deal, buddy, but that's all you got!
Lamarr Simms played by Don Stroud in Joe Kidd (1972)

DEALT HAND

I guess a man has got to play the cards he's dealt.
Matt Dillon played by James Arness in Gunsmoke: The Long Ride (1993)

59

DEATH

No one's ever gone until they're forgotten.
Brady Hawkes played by Kenny Rogers in <u>Gambler V: Playing for Keeps</u> (1994)

Death is nothing to one who does not fear it.
Kwai-Chang Caine played by David Carradine in <u>The Gambler Returns: The Luck of the Draw</u> (1991)

I would rather a swift death in battle against the whites than a slow death on their reservation.
Chief Looking Glass played by W. Vincent St. Cyr in <u>I Will Fight No More Forever</u> (1975)

I've been dying for a long time. Death is an old friend.
Judge Benson played by Edgar Stehli in <u>No Name on the Bullet</u> (1959)

Death is inevitable for all of us. But we all try to put it off for as long as possible.
Dr. Luke Canfield played by Charles Drake in <u>No Name on the Bullet</u> (1959)

You can never bet on how you would behave when death is staring you in the face.
Ambrose Bierce played by Gregory Peck in <u>Old Gringo</u> (1989)

It's easy to spit on a dead man.
Jet Cosgrave played by John Derek in <u>The Outcast</u> (1954)

We never know how close to us death may be hovering.
The Preacher played by William Shatner in <u>The Outrage</u> (1964)

Death is a trail we all have to ride. Sometimes it seems that it's leading us nowhere. But I got an idea it ends up in mighty pretty, green pastures.
Gene Autry played himself in <u>Saginaw Trail</u> (1953)

You can't lean on a dead man.
Dallas played by Ann-Margret in <u>Stagecoach</u> (1966)

Quantrell: Deathriders. I never really liked that name.

Roy: Why is that?

Quantrell: Because we ride in numbers; death rides alone.

General J.W. Quantrell played by Brion James and Roy Ackett played by Bo Svenson in Steel Frontier (1995)

Let the dead past bury its dead.

Harry Wringle played by Willis Bouchey in Two Rode Together (1961)

DEATH & ACCEPTANCE

The best thing you can do with death is ride off from it.

Captain Woodrow F. Call played by Tommy Lee Jones in Lonesome Dove (1989)

If death is coming, I'd just as soon meet it head on.

Josiah Sanchez played by Ron Perlman in The Magnificent Seven: The Series (1998)

I don't think a death ever goes down easy.

Steve Sinclair played by Robert Taylor in Saddle the Wind (1958)

DEATH & CERTAINTY

There's nothing certain except taxes and death.

Charley the Barber played by Clem Bevans in Dodge City (1939)

Never tally the dead before they're buried.

General Grey played by Anthony Zerbe in Independence (1987)

DEATH & DIAGNOSIS

Cyrus: Is he dead?

Undertaker: Graveyard dead.

Cyrus B. Bloomington played by James Coburn and the Undertaker/Jedediah played by Gregory Hines in The Cherokee Kid (1996)

He's deader than sagebrush.
Stony Brooke played by Robert Livingston in <u>Under Texas Skies</u> (1940)

DEATH & TIME
He was dead before God got the news.
Billy One-Eye played by Slim Pickens in <u>The Gun and the Pulpit</u> (1974)

There can be no haste before the eternity of death.
Reverend Pierce played by Claudio Gora in <u>The Hellbenders</u> (1967)

All I know is, when you're dead, you're dead a long time.
Justine Corley played by Harry Shannon in <u>Man or Gun</u> (1958)

DEBT
Living in debt is the American way.
Bret Maverick played by James Garner in <u>Bret Maverick: The Lazy Ace</u> (1981)

Debt's a funny thing. So much depends on whom you owe them to.
Doc Weber played by John Carradine in <u>Showdown at Boot Hill</u> (1958)

Being beholden always costs more in the end.
Major Rufus Cobb played by Frank Overton in <u>The True Story of Jesse James</u> (1957)

A law broke is a debt owed.
Charlie Siringo played by Steve Forrest in <u>Wanted: The Sundance Woman</u> (1976)

DECEPTION
I don't hold much for a sail under false colors.
Captain Elijah Bartlett played by Ferris Taylor in <u>Ridin' on a Rainbow</u> (1941)

DECIMAL POINT

I'm just as handy with a gun as I am with a pencil. I can make the same decimal point with either.
Avery played by Dan Duryea in The Marauders (1955)

DEEDS

We judge a man here by his deeds, not by his name.
Andrew Naab played by Robert Barrat in Heritage of the Desert (1939)

No good deed goes unpunished.
Amos Russell played by M.C. Gainey in The Last Cowboy (2003)

DEFEAT

There's no good place for defeat.
Sir Colin played by Patrick Macnee in The Gambler Returns: The Luck of the Draw (1991)

A fella once said, 'What is defeat? You go home!'
Weatherby played by Forrest Lewis in Gun Fury (1953)

DEPARTURE

Never look back, Billy, when you're leaving somewhere you don't want to see again.
Arch Deans played by Gregory Peck in Billy Two Hats (1973)

We're just as anxious to go as you are to get rid of us.
Sgt. Harper played by Robert Osterloh in Drums in the Deep South (1951)

I don't need no stone or log to fall on me to know it's time to go.
Peaceful Jones played by Charles Kemper in Fury at Furnace Creek (1948)

All I want is to be gone between me and here.
J.W. Coop played by Cliff Robertson in J.W. Coop (1971)

It makes a man feel good to have a woman watch him as he rides off.
Nicolai Gregorovitch Karakozeff played by Buddy Baer in <u>Jubilee Trail</u> *(1954)*

DEPENDENCY

We have come to need them [white men things]. That is our undoing, and it will be our ending.
Chomina played by August Schellenberg in <u>Black Robe</u> *(1991)*

Son: I can't abandon you, Mother.
Mother: You're not abandoning me. By going, you'll be taking care of me.
Rod Elliot played by Lukas Haas and Mrs. Elliot played by Dannette McKay in <u>Warrior Spirit</u> *(1994)*

DEPRECIATION

Chicken today, feathers tomorrow.
Jeff McCloud played by Robert Mitchum in <u>The Lusty Men</u> *(1952)*

DESPERATION

You're a man between a rock and a hard place looking for a way out.
Sam Brassfield played by Robert Taylor in <u>Cattle King</u> *(1963)*

People get desperate when their means of livelihood is cut off.
Gary Brannon played by Audie Murphy in <u>Drums Across the River</u> *(1954)*

Sometimes a man will do most anything when he's up against it.
Ace Cain played by Emmett Vogan in <u>Empty Holsters</u> *(1937)*

A drowning man grabs at straws.
Dan Ballard played by John Payne in <u>Silver Lode</u> *(1954)*

DESTINATION

Luke: Have you been here long?

Wood: Ever since I come.

Luke Matthews played by James Coburn and Wood Cutter played by Jerry Gatlin in Bite the Bullet *(1975)*

Where I'm from has nothing to do with where I'm going.

Nevada played by David Sharpe in Colorado Serenade *(1946)*

To know where you are going is to know where you will end.

The Piute Girl played by Susan Cabot in Fort Massacre *(1958)*

I didn't get where I am not knowing what I'm doing.

Mattie Baker played by Adrienne Barbeau in Ghost Rock *(2003)*

I made it a rule never to ask people where they've been, only where they're going.

Fairweather played by Frank Faylen in The Lone Gun *(1954)*

I go this way. You got a choice of three other directions.

Link played by Charles Bronson in Red Sun *(1971)*

The question is this: when is enough? When have you gone too far, and when have you not gone far enough? It's a hard question. Every road you go down, at some point you're going to say: is this leading to my destination or am I just getting more lost?

Samuel Clemens played by James Garner in Roughing It *(2002)*

Where you start from has nothing to do with where you finish, or how.

James "Doc" Underwood played by Lewis Stone in Three Godfathers *(1936)*

DESTINATION & SPEED

We could get there a lot faster, Captain, if we knew where we were going.

The Union Officer was uncredited in Kansas Raiders *(1950)*

You'll get where you're going quicker if you don't hurry so fast.
Kit Carson played by Jon Hall in <u>Kit Carson</u> (1940)

Speed is not as important as getting through.
Captain Gregson played by Harry Carey, Jr., in <u>Warpath</u> (1951)

DETERMINATION

I do know that if you want something badly enough, and if you work at it hard enough, well, most of the time you can make it happen.
Timothy Donovan played by Darren McGavin in <u>Donovan's Kid</u> (1979)

DIAGNOSIS

I pronounce him dead but not buried.
Dr. Speed played by Vince Barnett in <u>Big Jack</u> (1949)

He ain't much alive but he ain't dead either.
Fuzzy Q. Jones played by Al St. John in <u>Gentlemen with Guns</u> (1946)

He's just about alive.
Deputy Ward Kent played by Don Galloway in <u>Gunfight in Abilene</u> (1967)

DIFFERENCES

You don't think of differences when you're small.
Catherine Cantrell played by Felicia Farr in <u>Reprisal!</u> (1956)

We have a proverb: 'Though we are all made of the same clay, a jug is not a vase.'
Señor Espejo played by Florenz Ames in <u>Viva Zapata!</u> (1952)

DIPLOMACY

There's times when cool-headed thinking can do a lot more than a fighting spirit.
Jim Arnold played by Howard Lang in <u>Bar 20 Rides Again</u> (1935)

Hatfield: Diplomacy talks louder than guns.

Largo: And kills more people.

Hatfield played by Robert Strange and Largo played by William Haade in Desert Bandit (1941)

Diplomacy is the art of giving your enemy the victory and keeping the power for yourself.

General Mirbeau played by Henry Stephenson in Lady from Louisiana (1941)

DISAPPEAR

He just disappeared into thin air.

Soapy played by Roscoe Ates in The Westward Trail (1948)

DISAPPOINTMENT

You got to learn to put up with life's disappointments. I know it's hard, but you got to learn to do it.

John Henry Lee played by Willie Nelson in Once Upon a Texas Train (1988)

My Sunday School teacher used to say: 'You got to learn to swallow disappointment in this sad life.'

Fred C. Dobbs played by Humphrey Bogart in The Treasure of the Sierra Madre (1948)

DISASTERS

A famous judge once said: 'The three worst things that can happen to mankind are pestilence, famine, and mob rule.'

Sheriff Henry Plummer played by Preston Foster in Montana Territory (1952)

DISCIPLINE

My father used to say: 'If you raise your voice and it doesn't do any good, it's time to raise your hand.'

Jake Birnbaum played by Jack Kruschen in McLintock! (1963)

DISCOVERY

Open your eyes, Ebenezer! Who knows what you'll discover.
Ghost of Christmas Past played by Michelle Thrush in <u>Ebenezer</u> (1997)

You don't always have to go traveling to find what you're looking for.
Mary Lingen played by Donna Reed in <u>Gentle Annie</u> (1944)

Have you ever had the joy of finding something that you've been looking for all your life?
Terrall Butler played by James Mitchell in <u>The Peacemaker</u> (1956)

Lin: I think sometimes women know more about men than men know about women.
John: What you said is like a door to a house: you have to open it and see what's inside.
Lin Connor played by Ilona Massey and John Drum played by Rod Cameron in <u>The Plunderers</u> (1948)

You don't tell a man about a woman. He has to find that out for himself.
Rose Leland played by Arleen Whelan in <u>Ramrod</u> (1947)

DISCRETION

Do you know why I like you? Because you're deaf. And you got just enough sense to be blind too.
Doc Council played by George Kennedy in <u>Fools' Parade</u> (1971)

DISEASE

You can't shoot a damn disease.
Judge Roy Bean played by Ned Beatty in <u>Streets of Laredo</u> (1995)

DISGUST

There comes a time when you are so sick of yourself that you are ready to try anything to become someone else.
Scott Swanson played by Max von Sydow in <u>The Reward</u> *(1965)*

DISTANCE

Rio: How much further do we got to go?
Jed: Until we get there!
Rio played by Michael Delano and Jed Catlow played by Yul Brynner in <u>Catlow</u> *(1971)*

When you've traveled around as much as I did at that age, you learn not to let anybody get too close.
Ward McNally played by James Brolin in <u>Cowboy</u> *(1983)*

It's a long walk to the gallows tree.
John Morgan Candy played by Bob Campbell in <u>Five Guns West</u> *(1955)*

The shortest way is not always the quickest.
Cap played by Denver Pyle in <u>Gunpoint</u> *(1966)*

We'll put some country between us.
Sean Devlin played by Alan Scarfe in <u>Gunsmoke: One Man's Justice</u> *(1994)*

I've come too far to turn back now.
Jace played by Warren Oates in <u>Mail Order Bride</u> *(1964)*

I like my Indians at a distance, field glass distance.
Hogger McCoy played by Chill Wills in <u>Rock Island Trail</u> *(1950)*

A wise man keeps his distance.
Sabata played by Lee Van Cleef in <u>Sabata</u> *(1969)*

You can go further at a trot than you can at a gallop.
Nan Morgan played by Ella Raines in Singing Guns (1950)

It's easier to go around a rock than to jump over it. It's longer but it's easier. So in the end it is shorter.
Jules Vincent played by Stewart Granger in The Wild North (1952)

DISTRACTIONS

Mister, would you get those females out of here. It's hard enough putting up this [telegraph] wire with the Indians around.
The Telegraph Worker was uncredited in Heller in Pink Tights (1960)

DIVERSIONS

Men deprived of their diversions are inclined to get restless.
Daniel Wheeler played by Lance Henriksen in Into the West (2005)

DOCTORS

One thing I'll say for the Doc: he figures out good ways to get us killed.
Private Gottschalk played by Harvey Lembeck in The Command (1954)

The law requires a medical examination for a man before be can be hanged.
Doc Merriam played by Edgar Buchanan in The Man from Colorado (1948)

Doc: I wouldn't let a cold develop into pneumonia if I could help it.
Asa: Why not? You can't cure a cold, but sometimes you can cure pneumonia.
Dr. Luke Canfield played by Charles Drake and Asa Canfield played by R.G. Armstrong in No Name on the Bullet (1959)

Doc: You're not going to take my advice, is that it?
Cass: Taking advice isn't like taking pills, Doc.
Dr. Barlow played by Edward Platt and Cass Silver played by Robert Ryan in The Proud Ones (1956)

DOCTORS & GOD

Rebecca: The Lord may yet see fit to save him.

Doc: He might, though I can't say I believe He'd be doing the rest of us much of a favor.

Rebecca Yoder played by Naomi Watts and Dr. Lucas Henry played by David Carradine in The Outsider (2002)

If God had an ounce of sense, He'd send this case to hell before the day is out.

Dr. Lucas Henry played by David Carradine in The Outsider (2002)

DOCTORS & OPERATIONS

Doc: Are you especially attached to that leg, Sam?

Sam: Well, it's sort of attached to me.

Dr. Noah Banteen played by Carl Benton Reid and Sam Granger played by John Pickard in Stage to Tucson (1950)

They had a lot of trouble takin' out Spud Taylor's appendix; they had to kill him first.

Zach Little played by Otis Harlan in 3 Bad Men (1926)

DOCTORS & PATIENTS

Fay: A doctor shouldn't get too involved with his patients.

Jim: Does that go for nurses?

Fay Carter played by Adrienne Corri and Jim Sinclair played by Hugh O'Brian in Africa—Texas Style! (1967)

As long as men are hurt and shot and killed every day, my business is good.

Doc Quinn played by Emmett Lynn in Code of the West (1947)

There's nothing I can do for 'em after they're dead but fill out their death certificates.

Dr. Jim Haynes played by Ross Elliott in Desert of Lost Men (1951)

He'll be all right as soon as I get all those holes plugged up.

The Doctor was uncredited in Domino Kid (1957)

Doc: I'll see you in the morning.

Rig: That you will, Doc. The question is, will I see you?

Doc played by Robert Ernst and Rig Barrett played by Bo Hopkins in Shaughnessy (1996)

You got to be careful about squirming around like this. I'm liable to cut your nose off. A barber did that to a fellow once. He stuck it back on but he got it on upside down. Every time the fellow sneezed, he blew his hat off. And when it rained, he drowned. You got to be careful.

Doc Weber played by John Carradine in Showdown at Boot Hill (1958)

DOGS

Let this sleeping dog lie, son. Doggone it, I'm dog-tired. I'm tired of leading a dog's life and fighting like dogs and cats against cats and dogs. Young puppies are dogging my trail, trying to become top dog. I'm going to the dogs in a dog-eat-dog world, son.

The voice of Wylie Burp was James Stewart in An American Tail: Fievel Goes West (1991)

You don't get between a dog and his bone.

Quincey Whitmore played by Jack Palance in Chato's Land (1972)

Only treacherous dogs bite the hand that helps.

Deerslayer played by Lex Barker in The Deerslayer (1957)

If people are going to kick me, I'd rather be a dog than a man.

Myrl Redding played by John Cusack in The Jack Bull (1999)

If you lie down with dogs, you get up with fleas.

Larry Kimball played by Smith Ballew in Rawhide (1938)

If you want to run with the pack, you got to be one of the dogs.

Roy Ackett played by Bo Svenson in Steel Frontier (1995)

DOWN UNDER

I sure would like to see him under.
Farnum played by Tony Epper in <u>*Gunsmoke: Return to Dodge*</u> *(1987)*

Henry: Where's Running Moon?
Bill: She's gone under, Henry.
Henry Frapp played by Brian Keith and Bill Tyler played by Charlton Heston in <u>*The Mountain Men*</u> *(1980)*

I'm going under, ain't I?
Henry Frapp played by Brian Keith in <u>*The Mountain Men*</u> *(1980)*

DREAM CATCHER

They hang them out for babies and married couples. Bad dreams get caught in the web and good dreams go through.
Archie Grey Owl played by Pierce Brosnan in <u>*Grey Owl*</u> *(1999)*

DREAMS

I dream too, only I don't dream as big as you.
Sam Dent played by Glenn Ford in <u>*The Americano*</u> *(1955)*

But can we say to people who think that dreams are the real world, this one is an illusion?
Father LaForgue played by Lothaire Bluteau in <u>*Black Robe*</u> *(1991)*

Don't intrude into another man's dreams unless you're prepared to pay for the intrusion.
Captain Pharaoh Coffin played by George Coulouris in <u>*California*</u> *(1946)*

Dreams are teachers that tell us of paths to follow.
Grandpa/Old Pete Chasing Horse played by August Schellenberg in <u>*Dreamkeeper*</u> *(2003)*

I understand about dreams. I understand about waking up, too.
Henry Moon played by Jack Nicholson in <u>Goin' South</u> (1978)

A man cannot ignore his dream, but be sure it is your dream and not that of another.
Dogstar played by Gil Birmingham in <u>Into the West</u> (2005)

I'd rather have you spoil them [dreams] than someone else make them come true.
Helen Colby played by Jean Muir in <u>The Outcasts of Poker Flat</u> (1937)

I've been chasing something all these years that was never there.
Calla Gaxton played by Dorothy Malone in <u>Pillars of the Sky</u> (1956)

Lizzie: You're all dreams, and it's no good to live in your dreams.
Bill: It's no good to live outside them.
Lizzie: Somewhere between the two.
Lizzie Curry played by Katharine Hepburn and Bill Starbuck played by Burt Lancaster in <u>The Rainmaker</u> (1956)

Bill: I hope your dreams come true. I hope they do.
Lizzie: They won't. They never do.
Bill: Believe in yourself and they will.
Bill Starbuck played by Burt Lancaster and Lizzie Curry played by Katharine Hepburn in <u>The Rainmaker</u> (1956)

Newt: Captain, I'm moving on. This is your dream.
Woodrow: Ain't no reason it can't be your dream too.
Newt: It's the same reason you couldn't live a life you didn't decide on by yourself. I understand that now.
Newt Dobbs played by Rick Schroder and Woodrow F. Call played by Jon Voight in <u>Return to Lonesome Dove</u> (1993)

Don't be so disrespectful about dreams, Kate. They very often have significance.
Cole Gregory played by Dennis Hoey in <u>Roll on Texas Moon</u> (1946)

An old man must cling to his dreams as desperately as he clings to life.
Don Alejandro de le Vega played by George J. Lewis in <u>The Sign of Zorro</u> (1960)

The real sadness of a dream is its unfulfillment.
Dr. Julia Winslow Garth played by Greer Garson in <u>Strange Lady in Town</u> (1955)

You got to grow your own dream.
Lewton Cole played by James Coburn in <u>Wuterhole #3</u> (1967)

DRIFTERS

You're as loose as ashes in the wind.
Print Ritter played by Robert Duvall in <u>Broken Trail</u> (2006)

Anytime I button my coat, my trunk is packed.
Gabby played by George "Gabby" Hayes in <u>Colorado</u> (1940)

When you've been drifting all your life, well, it's just kind of hard to settle down in one place.
Sunset Carson played himself in <u>El Paso Kid</u> (1946)

I just got roamin' in my blood, I guess.
Kentucky played by Ken Maynard in <u>In Old Santa Fe</u> (1934)

I'm the drifting kind. I always like to know what's over the next hill.
Tom Crenshaw played by Tom Tyler in <u>Santa Fe Bound</u> (1936)

DRIFTING

Eddie: I got a hunch we better just let things drift along.
Roscoe: Sometimes things can drift too far.
Eddie Dean as himself and Soapy played by Roscoe Ates in <u>Driftin' River</u> (1946)

DRINKING

Whiskey for me and beer for my horse!
Carbo played by Jan-Michael Vincent in <u>Bite the Bullet</u> (1975)

I'm better at finding stuff if I'm drinking.
Jason played by Alan Shearman in <u>Black Fox: Good Men and Bad</u> (1995)

My daddy, he'd walk forty miles for liquor and not forty inches for kindness.
Ruby Thewes played by Renee Zellweger in <u>Cold Mountain</u> (2003)

I was giving mouth-to-mouth resuscitation to a bottle of tequila, and we lost her too!
Norman "Sonny" Steele played by Robert Redford in <u>The Electric Horseman</u> (1979)

I hate to drink a man's beer and then have him shot at sunrise.
Marshal Max Cooper played by John Doucette in <u>The Fastest Guitar Alive</u> (1967)

A man doesn't like to be stared at when he's drinking.
George Kelby, Jr., played by Glenn Ford in <u>The Fastest Gun Alive</u> (1956)

The only time to let out a yell or take a drink of whiskey is when you're alone or with somebody.
Big Boy Matson played by Woody Harrelson in <u>The Hi-Lo Country</u> (1998)

I know I shouldn't have sobered up. Something always happens when I do.
Dr. Denton played by Herbert Heywood in <u>Legion of the Lawless</u> (1940)

Any damn fool can drink himself to death.
Wild Bill Hickok played by Jeff Corey in <u>Little Big Man</u> (1970)

The fate of our nation must not be bandied over empty glasses.
Senator Claud Demmet played by Ed Begley in <u>Lone Star</u> (1952)

Tom: Are you gonna take a bath?

Cap: Well, I've been working from the inside out.

Tom Sunday played by Glenn Ford and Cap Roundtree played by Ben Johnson in The Sacketts (1979)

You're not going to solve anything by turning yourself into a whiskey bottle.

Dr. Jonathan Mark played by Walter Brennen in Singing Guns (1950)

What are you trying to do, drown yourself?

Billy Burns played by George "Gabby" Hayes in Trail Street (1947)

Bartender: What's wrong? Doesn't my rum agree with you?

Englishman: Oh yes; I was just coughing to make conversation.

The Bartender was uncredited and the Englishman, Lord Castlepool, played by Eddi Arent in The Treasure of Silver Lake (1962)

I never touch the rotten stuff except when I'm alone or with somebody.

Jennings played by Victor Buono in The Wrath of God (1972)

He was so drunk he couldn't hit the ground with his hat in three tries.

Ed Masterson played by Bill Pullman in Wyatt Earp (1994)

DROWNING

If you was to drown, they'd find your body upstream.

Dan Candy played by Donald Sutherland in Alien Thunder (1973)

It's a nice river to get drowned in; not too muddy.

Jed Hooker played by Ossie Davis in Sam Whiskey (1969)

DUE PROCESS

He'll hang by government rope.

Len Merrick played by Kirk Douglas in Along the Great Divide (1951)

Knowing something and proving it, that's two different things.
Marshal Cheyenne Davis played by Al "Lash" LaRue in <u>Law of the Lash</u> *(1947)*

DUMB

[He's] about twelve biscuits short of a dozen!
Bret Maverick played by James Garner in <u>Bret Maverick: The Lazy Ace</u> *(1981)*

He's too dumb to be anything but honest.
Sam L. Gorman played by Walter Miller in <u>Bullet Code</u> *(1940)*

Sergeant Garcia could not put together two pieces of bread to make a sandwich.
Capitan Monastario played by Britt Lomond in <u>The Sign of Zorro</u> *(1960)*

It seems there's such a thing as being so dumb it gets to be smartness.
Stag Roper played by Douglas Fowley in <u>20 Mule Team</u> *(1940)*

DUTY

I just do what has to be done. I don't have to like it.
Ed "Blackie" Dawson played by Charles King in <u>Ghost of Hidden Valley</u> *(1946)*

A man's got to do what he's got to do.
The Diesel Drive played by Bruce Kirby in <u>J.W. Coop</u> *(1971)*

Everybody has to do things they don't always like.
Preacher Bob played by Peter Boyle in <u>Kid Blue</u> *(1973)*

You're a peace officer. I'm sure that you understand about duty: 'I slept and dreamed that life was beauty. I woke, and found that life was duty.'
Eula Goodnight played by Katharine Hepburn, quoting poem "Life and Duty" by Ellen Struges Hoope, in <u>Rooster Cogburn</u> *(1975)*

Some things a man has to do so he does it.
Lin McAdam played by James Stewart in <u>Winchester '73</u> *(1950)*

DYING

Some people ain't got sense enough to die when they're supposed to.
The Henchman was uncredited in <u>Adios Amigo</u> (1975)

You'd like me to die quickly, wouldn't you, without wasting too much of your time? Or quietly, so I won't embarrass you too much? Or even thankfully, so your memory of the occasion won't be too unpleasant?
John J. MacReedy played by Spencer Tracy in <u>Bad Day at Black Rock</u> (1955)

If you have to go out, you might as well make it count for something.
Sheriff Cole played by Clark Howat in <u>Billy Jack</u> (1971)

I guess there's no good way to die.
J.D. Cahill played by John Wayne in <u>Cahill: United States Marshal</u> (1973)

You're a lucky man, son. Most men don't get to choose the time to die.
Sam Kendrick played by Stacy Keach in <u>Desolation Canyon</u> (2006)

He sure died nice.
The Bartender played by Olin Howlin in <u>Hellfire</u> (1949)

It's funny how different things look when you're lying flat on your back looking up.
Marshal Bucky McClean played by Forrest Tucker in <u>Hellfire</u> (1949)

Billy: It's not much of a place to die.
Wes: Is there a good one?
Billy played by David Dukes and Wes played by Paul Johansson in <u>Hooded Angels</u> (2000)

I don't like a lot of folks around me when I'm doing something important like dying.
Tom O'Folliard played by George Berkeley in <u>The Law vs. Billy the Kid</u> (1954)

Doc: Don't compare us. We've got nothing in common.
Gant: Everybody dies.
Dr. Luke Canfield played by Charles Drake and John Gant played by Audie Murphy in <u>No Name on the Bullet</u> (1959)

He ran out of breath.
Keeler played by Hugh Prosser in <u>The Phantom Rider</u> (1946)

There ain't no profit in dying.
Carver played by Blair Underwood in <u>Posse</u> (1993)

I sure wouldn't want to see anyone die unpleasant.
Gil Favor played by Eric Fleming in the premiere episode of <u>Rawhide</u> (1959)

It's funny how some people have to die before they learn how they should have lived.
Cap MacKellar played by Walter Brennan in <u>The Showdown</u> (1950)

One way or the other, you die at the end.
Willie Boy played by Robert Blake in <u>Tell Them Willie Boy Is Here</u> (1969)

It is a good day to die.
Windwalker played by Trevor Howard in <u>Windwalker</u> (1980)

DYING & FEAR

An Indian isn't afraid to die. Don't ever expect a white man to understand that.
Billy Jack played by Tom Laughlin in <u>Billy Jack</u> (1971)

Martha: Are you afraid to die?
Asa: Well, I can't exactly say I'm pleased about it.
Martha Knox played by Nina Guilbert and Asa Knox/Ace Carter played by Rex Lease in <u>Cavalcade of the West</u> (1936)

To be afraid means dying every day. A man who isn't afraid can only die once.
Montgomery Brown/Ringo played by Giuliano Gemma in <u>The Return of Ringo</u> (1966)

DYING & FIGHTING

He died with his face to the enemy.
MacDougall played by Wilfrid Lawson in <u>Allegheny Uprising</u> (1939)

A good soldier dies only once. And death is someone he knows.
General Johnston played by Lewis Martin in <u>Drums in the Deep South</u> (1965)

It's better to die fighting than lying with your face in the dirt.
Captain Bruce Coburn played by Audie Murphy in <u>40 Guns to Apache Pass</u> (1967)

I'm not going to die in bed if there's a good fight around.
James Ketchum played by James Philbrook in <u>Son of a Gunfighter</u> (1965)

DYING & TIMES

I've never died so many times in my whole life.
Luck Hatcher played by Michael Ironside in <u>Deadman's Revenge</u> (1994)

You can only die once.
Jenny "Ma" Grier played by Jane Darwell in <u>The Ox-Bow Incident</u> (1943)

EAST & WEST

If the East won't go to the West, we'll bring the West to the East!
Ned Buntline played by Thomas Mitchell in <u>Buffalo Bill</u> (1944)

East is east and west is west, but never between shall meet.
Kay Dodge played by June Storey, paraphrasing Rudyard Kipling, in <u>Rancho Grande</u> (1940)

EATING

I always speak Spanish when I'm eating. It gives it a better flavor.
Deputy Art Benson played by Guinn "Big Boy" Williams in <u>Brimstone</u> (1949)

Eating is not a spectator sport.
Narration by Winston Hibler in <u>King of the Grizzlies</u> (1970)

I don't eat things that are still moving.
Matthew Quigley played by Tom Selleck in <u>Quigley Down Under</u> (1990)

EDGE

An ace in the hole is a good thing to have sometimes.
Tex Haines played by Tex Ritter in <u>Flaming Bullets</u> (1945)

EDUCATION

Hopalong: I didn't know Ike could count above ten.
California: Not without taking his boots off, he can't.
Hopalong Cassidy played by William Boyd and California Carlson played by Andy Clyde in Forty Thieves *(1944)*

Sometimes I think that's getting to be the trouble with this country: too much education!
Colonel Chris Ferris played by Claude Rains in Gold Is Where You Find It *(1938)*

There's enough ignorance in the world without encouraging it in the classroom.
The Concerned Parent was uncredited in Lone Star *(1996)*

There is a saying, a very old saying: when the pupil is ready, the master will appear.
Don Diego de la Vega/Zorro played by Anthony Hopkins in The Mask of Zorro *(1998)*

Julie Ann: If you're talking sense, you manage to hide it behind a lot of educated words.
John: I went to school, and I learned to read. Don't hold it against me.
Julie Ann McCabe played by Adrian Booth/Lorna Gray and John Drum played by Rod Cameron in The Plunderers *(1948)*

Education is freedom.
King David Lee played by Robert Hooks in Posse *(1993)*

EFFICIENCY

You got to do the best with what you got while you got it.
Frank Post played by Ryan O'Neal in Wild Rovers *(1971)*

EFFORT

You can't get water out of a well without dipping in a bucket.
Daniel Boone played by Fess Parker in Daniel Boone: Frontier Trail Rider *(1968)*

We got a saying down in Texas that a fella doesn't get anyplace unless he tries.
Bob Seton played by John Wayne in <u>Dark Command</u> (1940)

Shakespeare said that if you run enough ropes through enough pulleys that you could lift the world.
Splinters played by Gordon Jones in <u>Spoilers of the Plains</u> (1951)

EGO

No matter how much I try to be otherwise, I'm just irresistible.
Jimmy Henderson played by Bob Steele in <u>The Oklahoma Cyclone</u> (1930)

ELUDING

You can't hide out from yourself.
Hollis Jarret played by Macdonald Carey in <u>Stranger at My Door</u> (1956)

EMPIRE

All the empire I ever really wanted was just a little corner somewhere for us.
Helen Colby played by Jean Muir in <u>The Outcasts of Poker Flat</u> (1937)

ENDURANCE

There are some things a man cannot bear.
Tom Jeffords played by James Stewart in <u>Broken Arrow</u> (1950)

What can't be cured must be endured.
Burton Standish played by John Anderson in <u>Scalplock</u> (1967)

ENEMY

Frank: You still have a lot of enemies in high places.
Pancho Villa: Yeah, that's the best place for enemies—high up where you can see them.
Frank Thayer played by Eion Bailey and Pancho Villa played by Antonio Banderas in <u>And Starring Pancho Villa as Himself</u> (2003)

In the absence of reliable information to the contrary, always assume that the enemy will act with good judgment.
General Paul De Marchand played by Hugo Haas in The Fighting Kentuckian (1949)

With most injuns, a tribe's greatness is figured on how mighty his enemies be.
Del Gue played by Stefan Gierasch in Jeremiah Johnson (1972)

There's an old saying among soldiers. When the Minie balls is flying and the artillery is hotter than hell, there's no such thing as an enemy.
Sgt. Mercer Barnes played by Noah Beery, Jr., in Journey to Shiloh (1968)

He's his own worst enemy.
Wil Jesse played by Ben Johnson in The Train Robbers (1973)

Never meet the enemy on his terms.
John Parrish played by Glenn Ford in The Violent Men (1955)

ENSLAVEMENT

Ladies, our enemy has two heads: first, the enslavement of women by men; and second, the enslavement of themselves by their remorseless tyrant—alcohol.
Cora Templeton Massingale played by Lee Remick in The Hallelujah Trail (1965)

EQUALITY

There's no rank. We're all equal, except for me being a little more equal.
Captain Rod Douglas played by George Peppard in Cannon for Cordoba (1970)

ESCAPE

Sheriff: Why did you escape for?
Tom: Because I could.
Sheriff Ed Smalley played by Richard Masur and Tom Horn played by David Carradine in Mr. Horn (1979)

EULOGY & EPITAPH

And may you be three days in heaven before the devil knows you're dead!
Joe played by Wilford Brimley in <u>Crossfire Trail</u> (2001)

I'd say a prayer for you, Frank. But coming from me, I'm afraid it's liable to do you more harm than good.
Ernie Parsons played by Marjoe Gortner in <u>The Gun and the Pulpit</u> (1974)

EVIDENCE

The first thing you learn in the law is you gotta catch 'em with the meat; the feathers don't count.
Sheriff Denning played by Frank Jenks in <u>Pecos River</u> (1951)

Sheriff: Innocent? You were caught leaving the town with the mayor's wife! You were riding stolen horses and you were carrying money taken from two bank holdups!
Matt: You call that evidence?
The Sheriff was uncredited and Matt Stone played by James Farentino in <u>Ride to Hangman's Tree</u> (1967)

EXCITEMENT

I figure a woman who shoots at me four times, I need to see her again.
Cherokee Kid/Isaiah played by Sinbad in <u>The Cherokee Kid</u> (1996)

EXCUSES

Excuses are a dime-a-dozen and not worth a plugged nickel.
Driscoll played by David Carradine in <u>Brothers in Arms</u> (2005)

EXILE

For the next four centuries, seeking gold, land or freedom, the white man spread relentlessly westward subjugating tribe after tribe. The Indian became an exile in his own land.
Narration in <u>I Will Fight No More Forever</u> (1975)

EXPANSION

Expansion is a mighty fine thing. Sure, we got to grow. But not at the expense of the things this country was founded on to protect.

Davy Crockett played by Fess Parker in Davy Crockett, King of the Wild Frontier *(1955)*

EXPECTATIONS

It's the things we least expect that usually happen.

Melgrove played by Edward Peil in Blue Steel *(1934)*

You shouldn't be so satisfied with so little. You've got a right to expect more.

Blaine Madden played by Rory Calhoun in The Gun Hawk *(1963)*

If you keep your expectations small, your disappointments won't be so big.

John Benton played by Tom London in Trail of Kit Carson *(1945)*

I'm not asking for any more than you can give me.

Josie Marcus played by Joanna Going in Wyatt Earp *(1994)*

EXPERIENCE

Nothing is a waste of time. It adds to the person that you are.

Clark Davis played by Dale Midkiff in Love Comes Softly *(2003)*

For your own good, the sooner you get your feet wet, the better.

Col. John Templeton played by Everett Sloane in Massacre at Sand Creek *(1956)*

You can sink or you can swim. Either way, you'll get wet.

Eben "McTooth" Campbell played by Donnelly Rhodes in Showdown at Williams Creek *(1991)*

EYES

I can see more in your eyes than words can tell me.

Hopalong Cassidy played by William Boyd in Cassidy of Bar 20 *(1938)*

For a young man with two bright eyes, you're mighty unseeing.
Sam Brannon played by Walter Brennan in <u>Drums Across the River</u> (1954)

FACES

Anyone with a face as ugly as yours should avoid looking in the mirror.
Colonel Greeley played by Cameron Mitchell in <u>The Gambler: The Adventure Continues</u> (1983)

A face like his belongs in a cemetery.
Felipe was uncredited in <u>A Pistol for Ringo</u> (1965)

FACTS

Facts have a way of changing, depending on who is issuing them.
Edward Janroe played by David Dukes in <u>Last Stand at Saber River</u> (1997)

FAILURE

A man doesn't like to be reminded of his failures.
Blaine Madden played by Rory Calhoun in <u>The Gun Hawk</u> (1963)

People don't go around admiring failures. There's too many of them.
Strain played by Jess Kirkpatrick in <u>These Thousand Hills</u> (1959)

FAIRNESS

I like people that shoot you from the front.
Johnny Lake played by Charles Drake in <u>Gunsmoke</u> (1953)

When you're gunning for a man, he deserves to die from the front and close enough to know the reason why.
Deputy Fenton played by Kieron Moore in <u>Son of a Gunfighter</u> (1965)

Everything's fair in love and war.
Brainard played by Ted Adams in <u>Straight Shooter</u> (1939)

FAITH

You can be whatever you want if you just believe in yourself.
The voice of Miss Kitty was Amy Irving in <u>An American Tail: Fievel Goes West</u> *(1991)*

I believe any faith within reach is worth reaching for.
Abraham Murdock played by James Griffith in <u>Heaven with a Gun</u> *(1969)*

Lt.: You can't do much with just faith.
Father: You can't do anything without it.
Lt. José Mendoza played by Richard Egan and Father Junipero Serra played by Michael Rennie in <u>Seven Cities of Gold</u> *(1955)*

Faith is an impregnable fortress.
Tobias played by Dan Sturkie in <u>They Call Me Trinity</u> *(1970)*

FAMILY

Family is all you got.
Elizabeth Kennedy played by Amy Jo Johnson in <u>Hard Ground</u> *(2003)*

My family is my life.
Alejandro/Zorro played by Antonio Banderas in <u>The Legend of Zorro</u> *(2005)*

Nothing counts as much as blood. Everybody else is just strangers.
Wyatt Earp played by Kevin Costner in <u>Wyatt Earp</u> *(1994)*

FASHION

Why should I be dressing you up for other men to look at?
Tom Conovan played by Bruce Cowling in <u>Ambush</u> *(1950)*

There's two times that a fellow ought to look his best: his wedding and his funeral.
Thunder Rogers played by Frank Rice in <u>Border Law</u> *(1931)*

Don't you know it takes two women to buy a dress?
Carla Forester played by Eleanor Parker in <u>*Escape from Fort Bravo*</u> *(1953)*

Josefa: We have a proverb: a man well dressed is a man well thought of.
Zapata: A monkey in silk is still a monkey.
Josefa played by Jean Peters and Emiliano Zapata played by Marlon Brando in <u>*Viva Zapata!*</u> *(1952)*

FATE & DESTINY

Where I'm going, I don't know what will become of me. But if I stay here, I know damn well what I'll become.
Liz Pickering played by Janice Rule in <u>*Alvarez Kelly*</u> *(1966)*

The destinies of men in many walks of life are controlled by the providence of others.
The Padre played by William Farnum in <u>*South of the Border*</u> *(1939)*

FATHERS

It's not enough just to plant the seed. A real father is a man who gives his whole life to the child.
Logan Keliher played by Audie Murphy in <u>*Bullet for a Badman*</u> *(1964)*

You ought to act more like a father and less like a warden.
Billy Roy played by Willie Nelson in <u>*Pair of Aces*</u> *(1990)*

FEAR

A man is not afraid of what's ahead of him, only what's behind him. The things that are worth living for, he's afraid of losing them.
Logan Cates played by Rory Calhoun in <u>*Apache Territory*</u> *(1958)*

A man's got to kill his own snakes.
Bickford "Bic" Waner/Kid Blue played by Dennis Hopper in <u>*Kid Blue*</u> *(1973)*

Most of the things we're afraid of never happen.
Cappy played by J. Farrell MacDonald in <u>Knights of the Range</u> (1940)

People are afraid of what they don't understand.
Alexandra Bergson played by Jessica Lange in <u>O Pioneers!</u> (1992)

Freedom to live without fear is man's most treasured possession.
Rev. Jericho Jones played by Charles "Buddy" Rogers in <u>The Parson and the Outlaw</u> (1957)

Fear is a deadly poison.
Rev. Jericho Jones played by Charles "Buddy" Rogers in <u>The Parson and the Outlaw</u> (1957)

If there's anything that scares the hell out of a fellow, it's a serious-talking girl.
Jim Curry played by Earl Holliman in <u>The Rainmaker</u> (1956)

We can't go on fearing tomorrow while today slips past us.
Jackson "Sugarfoot" Redan played by Randolph Scott in <u>Sugarfoot</u> (1951)

FEELINGS

You haven't any more feelings than a ten-minute egg.
Ann Kincaid played by Jane Wyman in <u>Cheyenne</u> (1947)

FENCES

Good fences make good neighbors.
Frank Madden played by Guy Madison in <u>Reprisal!</u> (1956)

A broken fence is an invitation.
Kit Barlow played by Peggy Stewart in <u>Trail to San Antone</u> (1947)

FIGHTING

Abe: It was a friendly fight.

J.D.: I've never been in one of them.

Abe Fraser played by George Kennedy and J.D. Cahill played by John Wayne in <u>*Cahill: United States Marshal*</u> *(1973)*

It's always been my contention that a good little man can whip an ordinary big man.

Clint Ross played by Don "Red" Barry in <u>*Days of Old Cheyenne*</u> *(1943)*

I'm not fighting against you; I'm fighting for them.

Zack Stone played by Richard Joseph Paul in <u>*Oblivion*</u> *(1994)*

Andy: Red Chief will fight to the death by old Hank's side.

Bill: Couldn't we just fight to the slight injury?

Andy Dorset played by Haley Joel Osment and Bill Driscoll played by Michael Jeter in <u>*The Ransom of Red Chief*</u> *(1998)*

I've found that a strong, agile, average man can nearly always beat a strong, clumsy, big man.

Alfie Alperin played by Malcolm McDowell in <u>*Sunset*</u> *(1988)*

We can be strong and skip a fight just as soon as win one.

The Virginian played by Bill Pullman in <u>*The Virginian*</u> *(1999)*

FIRE

Fire is hot without putting your finger in to find out.

Hopalong Cassidy played by William Boyd in <u>*Silent Conflict*</u> *(1948)*

FISHING

Fishing sure does take the miseries out of a man.

Big John McKay played by George Kennedy in <u>*The Good Guys and the Bad Guys*</u> *(1969)*

FLATTERY

Flattery and money will get you anything.

Rosie played by Jean Willes in Bite the Bullet (1975)

FLEXIBILITY

Sometimes you bend with the breeze, or you break.

Vin played by Steve McQueen in The Magnificent Seven (1960)

FLOWERS

Calem: And how is the flower of the west this morning?

Molly: Gone to seed.

Calem Ware played by Randolph Scott and Molly Higgins played by Ruth Donnelly in A Lawless Street (1955)

FOCUS

Let's get our cows over their buckets.

Judge Isaacs played by James Earl Jones in Sommersby (1993)

FOG

I like the fog. It shuts out the rest of the world.

Mary Smith played by Merle Oberon in The Cowboy and the Lady (1938)

FOOD

It makes me want to go home and shoot my Chinese cook.

Frederick Carson played by Paul Hurst in Angel and the Badman (1947)

Johnny: What does trout taste like?

Susie: Like chicken, only different.

Johnny Ears played by Franco Nero and Susie played by Pamela Tiffin in Deaf Smith & Johnny Ears (1972)

I've tasted worse but I don't know when.

California played by Andy Clyde in Wide Open Town (1941)

FOOD CHAIN

Everything dies. Flies get eaten by fish; fish get eaten by otters; otters get eaten by wolves. I've seen a bear kill a wolf and rip out its guts to eat. I've seen men kill bears. And I've seen a man three weeks dead covered in flies.
Archie/Grey Owl played by Pierce Brosnan in Grey Owl (1999)

FOOLS

A fool sees only today.
Tom Jeffords played by James Stewart in Broken Arrow (1950)

Nobody can make a fool out of a man except himself.
Johnny Wade played by Brian Keith in The Bull of the West (1971)

A fool and his money are soon parted.
Tim Holt as himself in Desert Passage (1952)

Only fools are so very sure.
Jo played by Rhonda Fleming in Gun Glory (1957)

FOR & AGAINST

It's better to have him for us than against us.
Trigger played by Lee Roberts in Driftin' River (1946)

FOREST

I love the forest because it's the last place men aren't in charge, the last wilderness.
Archie Grey Owl played by Pierce Brosnan in Grey Owl (1999)

Sometimes the forest can be deceptively peaceful, offering only an illusion of safety.
The Settler was uncredited in Last of the Mohicans (1977)

FORGIVENESS

An insulting remark, my friend, but I'll forgive you for it, remembering, as the Bard of Avon said so well, 'The quality of mercy is not strained.'
Fletcher played by John Carradine in <u>The Kentuckian</u> *(1955)*

There ain't no sense trying to peel the skin off a dead man.
Nip Hawkes played by Charles King in <u>The Lone Avenger</u> *(1933)*

That's a wife's profession, forgiving her husband.
Jeff McCloud played by Robert Mitchum in <u>The Lusty Men</u> *(1952)*

Winterhawk must be greater than his enemy. He must forgive them.
Clayanna played by Dawn Wells in <u>Winterhawk</u> *(1976)*

FORWARD

He isn't very backward about being forward, is he?
Diana Westcott played by Georgia Hawkins in <u>Doomed Caravan</u> *(1941)*

FOX

He who runneth with the fox must beware of the hounds.
Quentin Bartlett played by Richard Haydn in <u>The Adventures of Bullwhip Griffin</u> *(1967)*

FREEDOM

You keep trying to build a fence around her. I'm offering her a ladder.
Del Stewart played by William Bishop in <u>Overland Pacific</u> *(1954)*

People who have had freedom as long as we have sometimes take it for granted.
Peterson played by William Forrest in <u>Rage at Dawn</u> *(1955)*

If you care for someone, if you truly care for 'em, you got to set 'em free. But you always keep 'em in your heart. You see, that's where they live.
Clara Allen played by Barbara Hershey in <u>Return to Lonesome Dove</u> *(1993)*

Better beans and freedom than steak and slavery.
Joseph Lee played by Ossie Davis in The Scalphunters (1968)

You don't know what freedom is worth until you lose it.
Abigail "Abby" Martha Hale played by Paulette Goddard in Unconquered (1947)

The eyes of freedom will always see through the blindfolds of tyranny. And the bonds of oppression will always be broken by the muscles of liberty.
Charlotte Taylor Wilson played by Lauren Hutton in Zorro, the Gay Blade (1981)

FRIENDLINESS

Bic: Ain't there anybody friendly around here?
Bartender: I'm friendly! What the hell do you want?
Bickford "Bic" Waner/Kid Blue played by Dennis Hopper and the Bartender played by Bobby Hall in Kid Blue (1973)

FRIENDS

You know, truly, a man's greatest riches are his friends.
Banjo Hackett played by Don Meredith in Banjo Hackett: Roamin' Free (1976)

From this moment, wherever you go, whatever you do, you will always be Kemo Sabe—trusted friend!
Young Tonto played by Patrick Montoya in The Legend of the Lone Ranger (1981)

How do you expect to make friends when you go around shooting everybody you meet?
John Carson played by Bryant Washburn in Shadows on the Sage (1942)

Judge: A man don't know how many friends he's got until he dies.
Doc: Sometimes he makes more friends by dying than by anything else he ever done.
Judge Wallen played by Paul Maxey and Doc Weber played by John Carradine in Showdown at Boot Hill (1958)

I always figure you might as well approach life like everybody is your friend rather than nobody is.

Paden played by Kevin Kline in <u>Silverado</u> (1985)

A faithful friend is the medicine of life.

Journal Entry in <u>Showdown at Williams Creek</u> (1991)

FRIENDS & ENEMIES

The enemy of my enemy is my friend.

Captain Juan Seguin played by Jordi Molla in <u>The Alamo</u> (2004)

They say an enemy is only an injured friend.

Captain John Harling played by Adrian Pasdar in <u>Ghost Brigade</u> (1993)

We ain't gonna be friends. Let's just keep from being enemies.

Sarah Anders played by Patricia Clarkson in <u>Pharaoh's Army</u> (1995)

FUNERALS

The funeral is for the living.

Rev. Jonathan Rudd played by Robert Mitchum in <u>5 Card Stud</u> (1968)

A man doesn't get to attend his own funeral very often.

Billy the Kid played by Anthony Dexter in <u>The Parson and the Outlaw</u> (1957)

I don't like going to funerals, especially my own.

Nugget Clark played by Eddy Waller in <u>Savage Frontier</u> (1953)

FUTURE

Your future hasn't been written yet. No one's has. Your future is whatever you make it. So make it a good one!

Dr. Emmett Brown played by Christopher Lloyd in <u>Back to the Future: Part III</u> (1990)

GAINS & LOSSES

Life is a matter of timing. My loss is your gain.
Jack Fleetwood played by John Glover in Dead Man's Gun (1997)

GAMBLERS

Never leave a man busted.
Brady Hawkes played by Kenny Rogers in The Gambler (1980)

Do you know that gamblers say, 'easy come, easy go'? Do you know why they say it? Because nothing they get is worth keeping; nothing to give and nothing to get.
Tom Earley played by Stewart Granger in Gun Glory (1957)

[He] lost his entire fortune gambling in Monaco. That's much more dignified than losing it in a stupid business deal.
Bridget Curry played by Shannon Finnegan in The Other Side of the Law (1995)

GAME

There's no fun just winning the game when you're alone.
Sabina McDade played by Eleanor Parker in The King and Four Queens (1956)

GENEROSITY

Haig might not have had two nickels to rub together when I met him, but he spent those two nickels on me.
Edith Hanasain played by Charlene Tilton in Border Shootout *(1990)*

Ice in the winter. That's what I give away.
John Noble played by Pat McCormick in Mr. Horn *(1979)*

There's nobody as generous as people who have nothing.
Tom Bryan played by Rory Calhoun in The Treasure of Pancho Villa *(1955)*

GENTLEMEN

A gentleman always agrees with a lady.
Flo played by Maggie Pierce in The Fastest Guitar Alive *(1967)*

Fine clothes do not make the gentleman.
Ricardo played by Frank Sinatra in The Kissing Bandit *(1948)*

Gentlemen don't carry cash.
Allenby played by Shane Briant in Wrangler *(1989)*

GETTING ALONG

Jim: Being so close, I thought I'd drop out and see how you're getting along.
Pat: Oh, we're getting along fine. Why don't you follow suit and get along?
Jim Calvert played by Barton MacLane and Pat played by Pat Brady in Song of Texas *(1943)*

GHOSTS

Sometimes dead men leave ghosts behind them.
Juke played by George "Gabby" Hayes in Albuquerque *(1948)*

Tomorrow we will be like ghosts, like the spirit that comes in dreams with no earth to walk on.
The Indian Chief played by Enrique Lucero in <u>Buck and the Preacher</u> (1972)

Anyone who wasn't so stupid and ignorant would know there isn't no ghosts in the daytime.
Skinner Bill Bragg/Ambrose Murphy played by Wallace Beery in <u>20 Mule Team</u> (1940)

GIFT HORSE

Experience has taught me to look carefully at a gift horse.
Paul Regret played by Stuart Whitman in <u>The Comancheros</u> (1961)

Never look a gift horse in the mouth. When good fortune comes your way, just relax and enjoy it.
Alfred Billings played by Harry/Henry Morgan in <u>The Forty-Niners</u> (1954)

GIFTS

Charley: I can't take your locket.
Sue: It's not your choice when it's a gift.
Charley Waite played by Kevin Costner and Sue Barlow played by Annette Bening in <u>Open Range</u> (2003)

Men don't know what they want until you give it to them. Then when they get it, it's exactly what they always wanted.
Dallas played by Elizabeth Ashley in <u>Stagecoach</u> (1986)

GIRLS

Little girls are to be seen and not heard.
Tim Braddock played by Tim McCoy in <u>Bulldog Courage</u> (1935)

GIVE & TAKE

Guns take life. Land gives it.
Dutch played by Reiner Schoene in <u>The Gunfighters</u> (1987)

I don't mind giving something away, but nobody takes anything from me.
Dave played by Jack Lord in premiere episode of Have Gun—Will Travel (1957)

You want something, you got to give a little.
Charlie Veer played by Douglas Kennedy in Wyoming Renegades (1955)

GIVING

When you cast your bread upon the waters, it sure comes back to you.
The Uncle, paraphrasing a passage from the Bible, was uncredited in The Bronze Buckaroo (1939)

He that gives to the poor shall not lack for himself.
Elias Hobbes played by Wallace Ford in The Great Jesse James Raid (1953)

GLORY

Without blood, without tears, there is no glory.
General Antonio Lopez de Santa Ana played by Emilio Echevarria in The Alamo (2004)

One crowded hour of glorious life is worth an age without a name.
William Travis played by Patrick Wilson in The Alamo (2004)

I don't want anybody with me that's riding the glory road. They're too dangerous.
Devereaux Burke played by Clark Gable in Lone Star (1952)

GOD

No bullet will stop the work of God.
The Preacher/Major Welles played by Warren Oates in The Blue and the Gray (1982)

Sometimes you can't ask God to do everything. You got to pitch in yourself.
The Preacher played by Chill Wills in Gun Glory (1957)

The truth of God's love is not that He allows bad things to happen. It's His promise that He'll be there with us when they do.
Clark Davis played by Dale Midkiff in Love Comes Softly (2003)

Jed: I guess we'll get along without any help from the Lord.
Josiah: Well, folks can get along without eyes too, but they can't see.
Jed Isbell played by Alan Hale and Josiah Dozier Gray played by Joel McCrea in Stars in My Crown (1950)

GOLD

There's no such thing as wanting a little gold.
Asa played by Tom Heaton in Call of the Wild (1992)

I found that there was more gold in people's pockets than in their teeth.
Doc Holliday played by Jason Robards, Jr., (explaining why he left dentistry for gambling) in Hour of the Gun (1967)

Gold is where you find it.
Johnny Greer played by Zachary Scott in The Secret of Convict Lake (1951)

GOOD & BAD

God uses the good ones, and the bad ones use God.
Mattie Appleyard played by James Stewart in Fools' Parade (1971)

I like him because he's so good, and he likes me because I'm so bad.
Doll Brown played by Marie Windsor in Hellfire (1949)

People remember evil long after they've forgotten good.
The Morphinist played by Brad Hunt in The Journeyman (2001)

There's good and bad in all of us. Try to remember the good things.
Hannah Ferber played by Jarma Lewis in The Marauders (1955)

It takes a lot of strength and spirit to look through a man's hatred and still see his good.

John Red Eagle played by Tim Abell in <u>Miracle at Sage Creek</u> (2005)

I'll tell you a trick that sometimes is a big help. You start looking around for something good to take the place of the bad. As a general rule, you can find it.

Jim Coates played by Fess Parker in <u>Old Yeller</u> (1957)

Good riddance to bad rubbish!

Windy Halliday played by George "Gabby" Hayes in <u>Rustler's Valley</u> (1937)

I believe in the worst of us there is some good.

Kate "Ma" Conway played by Sarah Padden in <u>Song of Old Wyoming</u> (1945)

GOOD OLD DAYS

Billy: Do you remember the good, gone days?

James: Clearer and better every day I get older.

Billy Irvine played by John Hurt and James Averill played by Kris Kristofferson in <u>Heaven's Gate</u> (1980)

Tom: The good old days are gone.

Red: Now what the hell is that supposed to mean?

Tom: Just Indian talk.

Tom Black Bull played by Frederic Forrest and Red Dillon played by Richard Widmark in <u>When the Legends Die</u> (1972)

GOODBYE

I wish I had said more to my wife before she passed. This may be the last time she sees you in this world, Charley, or you her. So tell her whatever you can because she's entitled to more than your backside walking away.

Boss Spearman played by Robert Duvall in <u>Open Range</u> (2003)

GOODNESS

Sometimes being a good man isn't enough.
Charlie Poke played by Robert Fuller in <u>Bonanza: The Next Generation</u> (1988)

There's something good in everything, Ben. It's just a matter of finding the good and bringing it out.
Hollis Jarret played by Macdonald Carey in <u>Stranger at My Door</u> (1956)

GOSSIP

Saloons and barbershops are usually pretty good clearinghouses for gossip.
Steve Reynolds/The Durango Kid played by Charles Starrett in <u>The Fighting Frontiersman</u> (1946)

Say something out loud sometimes and it cuts down on the whispering.
The Preacher played by Chill Wills in <u>Gun Glory</u> (1957)

There's an old saying that a gossipy tongue is more dangerous than a gun.
Mayor John Blaine played by Paul Everton in <u>Gun Law</u> (1938)

He was in the lead when they were passing out the tongues.
Marshal Charlie Connelly played by Gene Evans in <u>The Last Day</u> (1975)

If you listen, you can hear anything.
Etta Place played by Katharine Ross in <u>Wanted: The Sundance Woman</u> (1976)

GOVERNMENT

Anyone who counts on government to do his job for him, well, he's a fool.
Ralph Holtz played by Chris Wiggins in <u>Black Fox: The Price of Peace</u> (1995)

One must look at government through the eye of a connoisseur, Juan. A government is like good food. Put in the right ingredients and you have a dish that sits well on everyone's stomach.
Don Arturo Bordega played by Cornel Wilde in <u>California Conquest</u> (1952)

That's the way the government does everything—the long way around.
The Townsman was uncredited in The Plunderers (1948)

Laws don't govern; men do.
Fernando played by Joseph Wiseman in Viva Zapata! (1952)

GRAVES

It's a very fine point of the law, but a man's grave is his castle.
Judge Higgins played by Karl Malden in The Adventures of Bullwhip Griffin (1967)

The rocks are more beautiful than any flower: all the colors of the rainbow and they never wither. When my time comes, that's what I want on my grave, not flowers.
Belle Starr played by Natalie Moorehead in Heart of Arizona (1938)

If a man ain't ready when he gets this far, a couple holies said over his grave ain't gonna help him none.
Clete played by Donald "Red" Barry in Seven Men from Now (1956)

You don't need to be a preacher to read The Book over a man's grave. All you need is a friendly feeling toward your fellow man.
Cap MacKellar played by Walter Brennan in The Showdown (1950)

GREED

A man's greed always leads him to his downfall.
The Professor played by Victor Kilian in Belle of the Yukon (1944)

The Lord saw fit to sprinkle gold on this land. And man and his greed is turning paradise into a pigsty.
Rev. Jonathan Rudd played by Robert Mitchum in 5 Card Stud (1968)

He'd sell his mother for two bits and give you change.
Jericho Howard played by James Millican in The Man from Colorado (1948)

Greed is a great magnet.
Sheriff Edward Gideon played by Eli Wallach in Shoot First ... Ask Questions Later! (1975)

GRIEF

I got grief enough on my own without taking on yours.
Will Lockhart played by James Stewart in The Man from Laramie (1955)

GRIEF & HAPPINESS

One man can bear grief. It takes two to be happy.
The Colonel played by Martin Landau in A Town Called Hell (1971)

GRIM REAPER

Cornelius: I could see death looking right at me, the Grim Reaper staring me right in the face.
Veronica: My, it must have been pretty horrible for both of you!
Cornelius J. Courtney played by Jimmy Durante and Veronica Whipple played by Barbara Jo Allen in Melody Ranch (1940)

GROUPS

A group without its leader has only half its strength.
Crawford played by Reed Hadley in The Half-Breed (1952)

GRUDGE

If there's one thing old Hoyce can carry, it's a grudge.
Jimbo played by Darren Dalton in Montana (1990)

GUNFIGHTERS

Close only counts when you're pitching horseshoes.
Cal Wayne played by Bobby Darin in Gunfight in Abilene (1967)

Do your thinking before you draw.
Martin Kanning played by Matt McCoy in Hard Bounty (1995)

It is possible to shoot a gun before you touch it. Of course, it takes lightning reflexes and considerable snake-eye concentration.
Jack Crabb played by Dustin Hoffman in <u>Little Big Man</u> (1970)

Gunfighters got no friends except other gunfighters.
Ed Bannister played by Peter Whitney in <u>Man from Del Rio</u> (1956)

Nobody likes to be told he can be out-shot. A man's got to find that out for himself.
Hugh Curdiff played by Sam Elliott in <u>Wild Times</u> (1980)

GUNFIGHTERS & GUNMEN

There's a difference between a gunfighter and a gunman. Now a gunfighter, well, he'll stand face-to-face with you and let you know what your chances are. Now a gunman, well, he'd just as soon shoot you in the front as he would in the back.
John Slaughter played by Michael Worth in <u>Ghost Rock</u> (2003)

GUNS

I got all the authority I need right here in my holster.
The Posse Member was uncredited in <u>The Avenging Rider</u> (1943)

God may have created man but Sam Colt made him equal.
Davis Healy played by Bruce Boxleitner in <u>Gunsmoke: One Man's Justice</u> (1994)

Men that don't carry guns usually live longer.
The Sheriff played by Hal Price in <u>The Last Horseman</u> (1944)

There is a lot of difference between a target and a man.
Banner Cole played by Audie Murphy in <u>Posse from Hell</u> (1961)

You can't argue with a gun.
Tom Owens played by Tyrone Power in <u>Rawhide</u> (1951)

I believe that carrying guns can get you into more trouble than they can get you out of.
Eddie Reed played by Eddie Dean in Song of Old Wyoming (1945)

A lot of people don't need a gun to make themselves heard.
Roy Carlin played by Victor Vilanova in The Texican (1966)

A gun will say a whole lot quick.
Tom Chaney played by Jeff Corey in True Grit (1969)

Learning to use a gun is not learning to kill.
Dan Corbin played by William Talman in Two-Gun Lady (1956)

GUTS

Harvey: I sometimes think I don't have the intestinal fortitude this job requires.
Zack: I think guts is the word, Harv. What you don't have is guts.
Harvey Burden played by Victor Buono and Zack Thomas played by Frank Sinatra in 4 For Texas (1963)

You think living life in a saddle makes you a man? It don't. It takes more guts sometimes to raise a family than it does to run off to the mountains.
Abner Murdock played by James Read in Walking Thunder (1997)

GYPSY

A gypsy without earrings is no gypsy at all.
Narita played by Dona Drake in Down Laredo Way (1953)

HABITS

I've never heard of a skunk changing his habits.
Jeff played by Raymond Hatton in <u>Come On, Rangers</u> *(1938)*

Old habits die hard.
Jason Cross played by Roger Rees in <u>The Return of Sam McCloud</u> *(1989)*

HALF-BREED

I want only peace between the two bloods that flow in my vein.
LeRoque/Wanechee played by George Lynn in <u>Saddlemates</u> *(1941)*

HANDS

I want him to know that there are two ways of putting out a hand. In a shake or a slap, you get back a hand accordingly.
Abigail "Abby" Taylor played by Frances Gifford in <u>American Empire</u> *(1942)*

The rich and powerful do not use their own hands.
Kwai Chang Caine played by David Carradine in <u>Kung Fu: The Movie</u> *(1986)*

Jeff: Preachers and politicians got to have the [hand] grip.

Preacher Sam: That's right. Folks like to know that their government and their church are in good, strong hands.

Jeff Shelby played by Jody McCrea and Preacher Sam Shelby played by Chill Wills in Young Guns of Texas *(1962)*

HANGING

They can't hang you any higher for two killings than they can for one.

Pete played by Spencer Williams in The Bronze Buckaroo *(1939)*

Hanging a woman tends to give a town a bad name.

Wichita Pike played by Ken Swofford in The Gambler: The Adventure Continues *(1983)*

Oh, the hood! We can place the rope over it or under it. Do you have a preference?

The Hangman played by Bill Catching in The Hanged Man *(1974)*

Give him enough rope and he'll hang himself.

Hoot played by Hoot Gibson in Outlaw Trail *(1944)*

Sheriff: Would you like to give us your names so we can tell your folks?

Guy: Our folks know our names.

The Sheriff was uncredited and Guy Russell played by Jack Lord in Ride to Hangman's Tree *(1967)*

Shoot me! Starve me! Even the knife! But do not use the rope. It would kill me to be hanged!

El Raton played by José Gonzales-Gonzales in The Three Outlaws *(1956)*

HAPPINESS

Happiness comes out of a struggle.

Betsy Bartlett McMasters played by Claudette Colbert in Boom Town *(1940)*

I've always tried to find peace in myself. It's not good to rely on people or things or new places to make you happy.
Clayton Drumm played by Fabio Testi in <u>China 9, Liberty 37</u> (1978)

Personally, I don't feel that getting myself shot is going to add to my happiness at all.
Bard Mackie played by Bruce Cabot in <u>Gunfighters</u> (1947)

There are certain people in this world who create happiness wherever they go; and there are others who create happiness whenever they go.
Mark Twain played by Christopher Connelly in <u>The Incredible Rocky Mountain Race</u> (1977)

When you love somebody enough, the thing you want to give most is happiness.
Captain John C. Fremont played by Dana Andrews in <u>Kit Carson</u> (1940)

You won't find no happiness on a road map. You got to bring it with you.
Billy Roy played by Willie Nelson in <u>Pair of Aces</u> (1990)

HARMONY

It's amazing what a little harmony will do.
Davy Crockett played by Billy Bob Thornton in <u>The Alamo</u> (2004)

When we perceive the ways of nature, we remove conflict within ourselves and discover a harmony of body and mind in accord with the flow of the universe.
Master Kan played by Philip Ahn in <u>Kung Fu</u> (1972)

HATE

Hate keeps me going. Hate is my weapon.
Jonas Steele played by Stacy Keach in <u>The Blue and the Gray</u> (1982)

There's nothing inside me but hate. Until I get rid of it, there's room for nothing else.
Daniel Halliday played by Joseph Cotton in <u>The Halliday Brand</u> (1957)

III

People cannot sing with hatred in their hearts.
The Boatman played by Victor Kilian in <u>The Mark of Zorro</u> (1940)

Hating never changes that which is already done.
The Padre played by Leander De Cordova in <u>The Mysterious Desperado</u> (1949)

There ain't nothing I like better than hate.
Rawhide played by Slim Whitaker in <u>The Oklahoma Cyclone</u> (1930)

Don't let your hate consume you.
Turtle Mother played by Tantoo Cardinal in <u>Tecumseh: The Last Warrior</u> (1995)

HEADQUARTERS

Capt.: Where's headquarters?
Sgt.: Wherever I'm standing.
Capt. Hank Tucker played by Scott Hylands and Sgt. Edgar Millen played by Lee Marvin in <u>Death Hunt</u> (1981)

HEADS & TAILS

Heads, I go first. Tails, you go second.
Luke played by David Wenham in <u>Dust</u> (2001)

HEALING

You get over things. It takes time but you get over them.
Lucy Antrim played by Abby Dalton in <u>Cole Younger, Gunfighter</u> (1958)

HEALTH

Nugget: How are you feeling, Howard?
Howard: Every year of my age!
Nugget Clark played by Eddy Waller and Howard Sanders played by Cliff Clark in <u>Vigilante Hideout</u> (1950)

HEARING

No matter how big a jackass' ear is, he cannot hear if it is filled with sand. Maybe you should shake the sand out of your ear.
Don Carlos played by Julian Rivero in <u>Riddle Ranch</u> *(1936)*

HEART

Don't let your heart rule your head.
Ace Crandall played by Robert Shayne in <u>The Dakota Kid</u> *(1951)*

What's the cash value of a heart of gold?
Matilda Boggs played by Patricia Knox in <u>Gentlemen with Guns</u> *(1946)*

Didn't anyone ever tell you that a sour heart leads to a sour face?
The Widow played by Amanda Donohoe in <u>Hooded Angels</u> *(2000)*

HEAVEN

Heaven is not out there. The other world is here.
Billy Jack played by Tom Laughlin in <u>Billy Jack</u> *(1971)*

Wyatt: What's your idea of heaven?
Josephine: Room service.
Wyatt Earp played by Kurt Russell and Josephine Marcus played by Dana Delany in <u>Tombstone</u> *(1993)*

HELL

You can bet there won't be any church bells ringing where you're going.
Quentin Leech played by Kenny Rogers in <u>Rio Diablo</u> *(1993)*

HELP

There are a lot of things you can do to help besides just standing around looking.
Linda Carter played by Marion Burns in <u>Paradise Canyon</u> *(1935)*

If you're not going to help, don't hinder!
Johnny played by Russ Tamblyn in <u>Son of a Gunfighter</u> (1965)

We can't help you unless you're willing to help yourself.
Tim Barrett played by Tim McCoy in <u>The Western Code</u> (1932)

HEROES

Maybe a real hero is the last one to hear about it.
James Stewart was the voice of Wylie Burp in the animated film <u>An American Tail: Fievel Goes West</u> (1991)

Dead heroes is coming too cheap these days.
Bill Satterwhite played by Robert Keith in <u>Drum Beat</u> (1954)

HICKS

You may think we're just a bunch of hicks. But hicks stick together!
Nels Oleson played by Richard Bull in <u>Little House: The Last Farewell</u> (1984)

HIDING

You can't hide forever.
Jim Hadley played by Alan Ladd in <u>Guns of the Timberland</u> (1960)

HINDSIGHT

Your hindsight is great!
Lt. Colonel John Hudson played by Paul Kelly in <u>Springfield Rifle</u> (1952)

HISTORY

History is written by those who win the battles.
Robert Wheeler played by Warren Kole in <u>Into the West</u> (2005)

History is a funny thing. They got us believing that Columbus discovered America, and the Indians were already here. That's like me telling you, and

you're sitting in your car, that I discovered your car. Then they want to call them the 'evil red savages' because they didn't give up the car soon enough.
The Storyteller played by Woody Strode in Posse (1993)

It's the little accidental things that sometimes change the course of history.
Lt. Colonel John Hudson played by Paul Kelly in Springfield Rifle (1952)

Thomasine: I wonder what history is going to say about us.
Bushrod: I guess it just depends on who writes it.
Thomasine played by Vonetta McGee and Bushrod played by Max Julien in Thomasine & Bushrod (1974)

HOGS

Hogs always want what's on the other side of the fence.
Alexandra Bergson played by Jessica Lange in O Pioneers! (1992)

If a hog could whisper in your ear, do you know what she would say? She would say, 'Just because I am ugly does not mean I like to be filthy.'
Ivar played by Tom Aldredge in O Pioneers! (1992)

HOLES

You dug this hole. As far as I'm concerned, you can crawl out of it yourself.
Virgil Renchler played by Orson Welles in Man In the Shadow (1957)

I feel like I could dig a hole and crawl into it and pull the hole in after me.
Phil Acton played by Paul Kelly in When a Man's a Man (1935)

HOME

Bartender: Why don't you go home?
Jake: I can't. The dog is in it.
Bartender Joe played by Richard Cramer and Jake played by Steve Clark in Arizona Stagecoach (1942)

Wherever I am is your home.
Chief Quanah Parker played by Kent Smith in <u>Comanche</u> (1956)

Home is where the heart is.
Captain John C. Fremont played by Dana Andrews in <u>Kit Carson</u> (1940)

I've lived with relatives my whole life: always a mansion but never a home.
Lorabelle Larkin played by Virginia Grey in <u>Slaughter Trail</u> (1951)

HONESTY

The worst an honest man can do is make an honest mistake.
Newt Dobbs played by Rick Schroder in <u>Return to Lonesome Dove</u> (1993)

HONOR

I guess there's nothing more pig-headed in a man than his sense of honor. They're all the same, every one of them. You take my Cleve now. He never could turn down a poker game. They're duty bound to go.
Lilith Prescott played by Debbie Reynolds in <u>How the West Was Won</u> (1962)

There is nothing in life worth more than honor.
Captain Juan Hernandez played by Conrad Parham in <u>The Proud and the Damned</u> (1972)

HOPE

Hope is a fever. It makes the eyes bright and the heart lighter. It makes the blood sing.
Willie Duggan played by Dan Duryea in <u>The Bounty Killer</u> (1965)

Hope is always around the corner.
Priscilla Lock played by Cecil Cunningham in <u>Cowboy Serenade</u> (1942)

Life is precious. The last thing any one of us wants to give up is hope.
Brady Hawkes played by Kenny Rogers in <u>Gambler V: Playing for Keeps</u> (1994)

Years pass, a small town and all, and your hopes begin to fade a little every day until you hardly remember what they were.
Sue Barlow played by Annette Bening in <u>Open Range</u> *(2003)*

Never say die.
Kay Harkrider played by Dale Evans in <u>Trigger, Jr.</u> *(1950)*

Remember, every cloud has a silver lining.
Ollie played by Oliver Hardy in <u>Way Out West</u> *(1937)*

HORN

Give a man a horn and he'll blow it.
Bye played by Ted De Corsia in <u>The Outriders</u> *(1950)*

HORSES

The wild horse—rough, tough, untamed and almost tireless—might well stand as a symbol for the Great American West.
Steve Reynolds/The Durango Kid played by Charles Starrett in <u>Cyclone Fury</u> *(1951)*

I'm counting on you to make a good pony out of that colt. And let it make a man out of you.
Rob McLaughlin played by Preston Foster in <u>My Friend Flicka</u> *(1943)*

Let's get some horses under us!
Gene Autry played himself in <u>Robin Hood of Texas</u> *(1947)*

I am like a wild horse. You can't tame me. You put the oats in the pen, though, and I'll come in for a nibble every day.
Roy O'Bannon played by Owen Wilson in <u>Shanghai Noon</u> *(2000)*

The wild horse is about the last living part of the Old West.
Chuck Reese played by Richard Farnsworth in <u>Wild Horses</u> *(1985)*

HOSPITALITY

People can say goodbye to you before you can say hello.
Jim Fallon played by Kirk Douglas in <u>The Big Trees</u> (1952)

When I offer my hospitality, it has no price.
Carla Ross played by Beth Brickell in <u>Posse</u> (1975)

HUMAN RACE

You look around at the human race and you got to wonder what the hell God was thinking about.
Ben Rumson played by Lee Marvin in <u>Paint Your Wagon</u> (1969)

HUNGER

The Cherokee have a saying: 'When the stomach is empty you may as well feed on sorrow.'
Mingo played by Ed Ames in <u>Daniel Boone: Frontier Trail Rider</u> (1968)

HUNTING

There's a difference between hunting and killing, you know.
Hunter Kirk played by James Duval in <u>The Doe Boy</u> (2001)

HURT

Clyborne: Is he hurt bad?
Marshal: Did you ever hear of anybody being hurt good?
Clyborne played by Roy Barcroft and the Marshal played by Grant Withers in <u>Old Los Angeles</u> (1948)

Jill: A girl's tears dry pretty quick.
Luke: How quick does blood stop flowing from a wound?
Jill Crane played by Carole Mathews and Luke Welsh played by Charles Bronson in <u>Showdown at Boot Hill</u> (1958)

I J

IDEALS

An Ideal isn't worth a penny if it isn't put to work.
Senator Blakely played by Ward Bond in Dakota Incident (1956)

It is much easier for a woman to be persuaded to forsake her ideals.
Captain Gutierrez played by Carlo Alighiero in The Five Man Army (1969)

The American Civil War was waged for a great ideal. But hardly had the smoke of battle cleared before that ideal was forgotten.
Prologue in The Texans (1938)

IDEAS

Hannibal: Well it could have been a lot worse.
Kid: How?
Hannibal: It could have been my idea?
Hannibal Hayes played by Peter Duel and Kid Curry played by Ben Murphy in Alias Smith and Jones (1971)

Never let your ideas shrink.
John Rutherford played by Harry Shannon in The Marauders (1955)

He gets a crackpot idea now and then. It's like the measles. You have to sit and wait until it wears itself out.
Billy Carson played by Larry "Buster" Crabbe in <u>Overland Riders</u> (1946)

Good ideas are hard to kill.
Hopalong Cassidy played by William Boyd in <u>Wide Open Town</u> (1941)

IDENTITY

You can't help being you, and I can't help being me.
Colonel Jim Bowie played by Richard Widmark in <u>The Alamo</u> (1960)

You have to find that there's something bigger and better in this world than being somebody else's cousin.
Poker Alice Moffit played by Elizabeth Taylor in <u>Poker Alice</u> (1987)

It's lonely trying to be something that you are not.
Matara played by Ralph Moody in <u>Reprisal!</u> (1956)

You can't be all things to all people.
Peter B. Clifford played by J.D. Cannon in <u>The Return of Sam McCloud</u> (1989)

IDIOTS

That sub-marginal idiot! Why, if he had twice as many brains as he had, he'd still be a half-wit.
Dr. J.D. Manning played by William Forrest in <u>Spoilers of the Plains</u> (1951)

God protects fools and drunks but not idiots.
Jennings played by Victor Buono in <u>The Wrath of God</u> (1972)

IDLENESS

The devil finds mischief for idle hands.
Dr. Clint Judson played by Grandon Rhodes in <u>On Top of Old Smoky</u> (1953)

IFs

There's not enough time in the day to stop and measure all the ifs.
Sheriff Edwards played by Edgar Buchanan in Edge of Eternity (1959)

IGNORANCE

Maybe I ain't as smart as some, but I'm always glad to add to my ignorance.
Corky McGee played by John Qualen in Belle Le Grande (1951)

Sometimes the less you know about a person, the better off you are.
Clare played by Kathleen Hughes in Dawn at Socorro (1954)

You look more natural just being ignorant.
Gabby Whitaker played by George "Gabby" Hayes in Don't Fence Me In (1945)

IGNORING

When a man makes a point of ignoring you, he ain't ignoring you at all.
H.C. Curry played by Cameron Prud'Homme in The Rainmaker (1956)

IMAGINATION

Don't let your imagination run away with you.
Billy Carson played by Larry "Buster" Crabbe in Border Badmen (1945)

You are a victim of your own imagination.
Jeffrey Carson played by George O'Brien in Hollywood Cowboy (1937)

IMITATION

That was a one-hundred-percent genuine imitation.
Gabby Whitaker played by George "Gabby" Hayes in Don't Fence Me In (1945)

IMMIGRATION

We don't feed our civilization to immigrants, we feed immigrants to our civilization.
Captain William H. Pratt played by Keith Carradine in Into the West (2005)

IMPORTANCE

I don't reckon it makes no never mind no more.
John T. Coleman played by John Clark Gable in <u>Bad Jim</u> (1990)

I thought I was a big duck. But I guess I'll have to hunt me a smaller puddle.
Bill Barker played by Harry Carey in <u>The Law West of Tombstone</u> (1938)

IMPRESSIONS

You just can't buy your way out of a bad impression.
Jim Kane played by Paul Newman in <u>Pocket Money</u> (1972)

IMPRISONMENT

You know, fifteen years of hard labor sort of cuts into your social life.
Cacopoulos played by Eli Wallach in <u>Ace High</u> (1967)

IMPULSIVENESS

What's the sense of being young if you can't be impulsive now and then, huh?
Spur played by Kirk Douglas in <u>The Man from Snowy River</u> (1982)

INDIAN PRAYER

Your life will be long. The good things will be yours. The sun will shine for you.
Sonseeahray/Morning Star played by Debra Paget in <u>Broken Arrow</u> (1950)

INDIANS

You can't be certain from a single arrow that the whole tribe is hostile.
Major Lowden played by Frank M. Thomas in <u>Apache Trail</u> (1942)

Well, that's a nice social problem: an Indian in the family!
Donna Cravat played by Nancy Dower/Judith Barrett in <u>Cimarron</u> (1931)

Nobody cares how much blood runs through a deer. But everyone wants to know how much blood runs through an Indian. It's kind of hard to tell unless you cut one of us open.
Marvin Fishinghawk played by Gordon Tootoosis in The Doe Boy (2001)

The only thing more pathetic than Indians on TV is Indians watching Indians on TV.
Thomas Builds-the-Fire played by Evan Adams in Smoke Signals (1998)

There are different kinds of Indians. But all Indians look alike in war paint and feathers.
Cactus Jack played by Joe Sawyer in The Traveling Saleswoman (1950)

Diseases have killed many more Indians than bullets.
President Duquesne played by Ron Glass in Unbowed (1999)

INDIANS & WHITE MEN

Killing a white man is a delicate matter.
Stone Calf played by Jimmy Herman in Dances With Wolves (1990)

White man wants all the ground and sky there is. And when he has it, he sleeps on beds so he cannot feel the ground, and puts roofs over his head so he cannot touch the sky.
Chief Shingiss played by Pedro de Cordoba in When the Redskins Rode (1951)

INITIATIVE

We just have to put one foot in front of the other.
Amos Russell played by M.C. Gainey in The Last Cowboy (2003)

INSIGHT

You can't even see what your own eyes show you.
Loved by the Buffalo played by George Leach in Into the West (2005)

There is sight and then there is insight.
Kulakinah played by Wes Studi in The Lone Ranger (2003)

INSULTS

Curley Tom: I've taken all the insults I'm gonna take from you!

Chick: I never said a word!

Curley Tom: Well, you looked something!

Curley Tom played by Paul Hurst and Chile "Chick" Lyman played by Noah Beery, Jr., in Bad Lands (1939)

INTENTIONS

The road to hell is paved with good intentions.

Jack Fowler/Jack Cole played by Randy Travis in The Long Ride Home (2003)

What a man intends and what he does is not always the same.

Ben Lane played by Audie Murphy in Six Black Horses (1962)

INTUITION

You just know some things without being told.

Rose of Sharon played by Maureen McCormick in Pony Express Rider (1976)

INVOLVEMENT

Are we to be moved by cruelty and injustices only when it touches us?

Don Miguel played by Alfonso Tafoya in The Mark of Zorro (1974)

IRISH

Poetry and piss and vinegar are the trinity of the Irish man.

Devin O'Neil played by Clive Owen in Class of '61 (1993)

ITCH & SCRATCH

Senator: Why are you scratching yourself all the time for?

Scratchy: Because I'm the only one that knows where it itches.

Senator Windblower played by Tom Leffingwell and Scratchy played by Philip Arnold in Buffalo Bill Rides Again (1947)

JACKASSES

Just because a mule don't see hisself as a jackass don't mean it ain't so. He is what he is.
Lucius played by Andre Braugher in Class of '61 *(1993)*

Act like jackasses and you'll be treated like 'em.
Owen Daybright played by Burt Lancaster in Vengeance Valley *(1951)*

JAIL

Breaking into jail is the easiest thing a fella can do.
Jack Burns played by Kirk Douglas in Lonely Are the Brave *(1962)*

JEALOUSY

Brett: If you give me your address, I'll send you a wedding gift.
Rannah: I'd rather you didn't.
Brett: Afraid your husband might misunderstand?
Rannah: Men always do.
Brett Wade played by Rory Calhoun and Rannah Hayes played by Piper Laurie in Dawn at Socorro *(1954)*

JOBS

The only way to do any job is to do it right.
Grandpa Culver played by Burr Caruth in Calling Wild Bill Elliott *(1943)*

I'm looking for a job with no work and big pay.
Chito Rafferty played by Richard Martin in Indian Agent *(1948)*

I never like to do half a job when the whole job's easier.
Johnny Crale played by Ned Young in Terror in a Texas Town *(1958)*

JOURNEY

Red Hawk: In its hurry to reach the shiny river, the mountain brook makes many mistakes.

Frances: But all the time it knows where it's going. And nothing can keep the brook and the river apart for long.
Red Hawk played by Philip Reed and Frances Oatman played by Ellen Drew in <u>Davy Crockett, Indian Scout</u> (1950)

His untimely death means that one journey is over and another has just begun.
Rev. Johnson played by Nick Scoggin in <u>Love Comes Softly</u> (2003)

JUDGMENT

'Judge not lest you be judged.' Matthew, first chapter, seventh verse.
Charlie Ledbetter played by Barry Corbin in <u>The Journeyman</u> (2001)

Question not a man until thee has examined his actions and found them simple.
Brother Abraham played by Robert Warwick in <u>Shoot-Out at Medicine Bend</u> (1957)

JUMPY

Measles couldn't even light on you. You're too wiggly.
Zeb Bascomb played by Wallace Beery in <u>Bad Bascomb</u> (1946)

JUSTICE

Sometimes justice can be very loud.
Pancho Villa played by Antonio Banderas in <u>And Starring Pancho Villa as Himself</u> (2003)

The scales of justice hang in a very delicate balance. There's nothing like money to tilt it our way.
The Judge played by Stephen Chase in <u>The Lawless Breed</u> (1952)

Justice doesn't need a courthouse or trappings of any kind, only order and truth.
The Judge played by Thomas Chalmers in <u>The Outrage</u> (1964)

KILLERS

When you come right down to it, all men in their hearts are killers.
Brendan O'Malley played by Kirk Douglas in <u>The Last Sunset</u> (1961)

I never met a killer yet that didn't say he was innocent.
Steve Howard played by Monte Hale in <u>Ranger of Cherokee Strip</u> (1949)

KILLING

I don't believe in unnecessary killing.
Bill Doolin played by Audie Murphy in <u>The Cimarron Kid</u> (1951)

There are ways of killing a man that don't break no law.
Sheriff Tomas "Swede" Lundstrom played by Patrick Duffy in <u>Desolation Canyon</u> (2006)

We don't kill the things we love.
Roger "Duke" Chadwick played by Kent Taylor in <u>Frontier Gambler</u> (1956)

I can teach you to hit what you aim at, but I can't teach you to kill what you shoot at.
Owen Pentecost played by Robert Stack in <u>Great Day in the Morning</u> (1956)

When the law kills, it's not murder; it's punishment.
Sheriff Gideon Burnett played by Frank Wolff in The Great Silence (1969)

I killed people because I thought taking other people's lives would somehow lengthen my own.
Johnny Lowen played by Harvey Keitel in Gunslinger's Revenge (2005)

Mordecai: What about after, what about after we do it [killing]?
The Stranger: Huh?
Mordecai: What do we do then?
The Stranger: Then you live with it.
Mordecai played by Billy Curtis and the Stranger played by Clint Eastwood in High Plains Drifter (1973)

A killing is a killing and there's no tying a pink ribbon on it.
Jim Bowie played by Alan Ladd in The Iron Mistress (1952)

Killing is one thing; hunting is another.
Matthew Thurston played by David Loden in Kid Vengeance (1977)

I'm not going to watch my two best friends kill each other even if I have to kill them myself.
Wyatt Earp played by Bruce Cowling in Masterson of Kansas (1954)

The ladies deprecate killing but, my, how they admire a war hero.
Grant Callum played by Dean Jagger in Pursued (1947)

Spurs: Nineteen years old and he's killed nineteen men. The trouble with Billy, he's too sensitive. You'd never know how many people don't understand him.
Doc: Well, offhand, I can think of at least nineteen!
Spurs O'Brien played by Lois Smith and Dr. Julia Winslow Garth played by Greer Garson in Strange Lady in Town (1955)

It takes two to make a killing.
Cinnabar played by Harry Woods in <u>Sunset Pass</u> *(1946)*

KISSING
Never kiss a girl on another girl's ranch.
Ed Garry played by Jon Hall in <u>Deputy Marshal</u> *(1949)*

Johnny: Don't I get a kiss goodbye?
Miss Baker: Well, we hardly know each other. I mean, I....
Johnny: Well, then, we'll make it a hello kiss.
Johnny Reach played by Dennis Cole and Miss Baker played by Melodie Johnson in <u>Powderkeg</u> *(1971)*

Kathleen: Aren't you going to kiss me goodbye?
Kirby: I never want to kiss you goodbye, Kathleen.
Mrs. Kathleen Yorke played by Maureen O'Hara and Lt. Colonel Kirby Yorke played by John Wayne in <u>Rio Grande</u> *(1950)*

KNOWLEDGE
It's not what you know. It's what you do with what you know that determines what kind of man you are.
Laura Fowler played by Vaughn Taylor in <u>The Long Ride Home</u> *(2003)*

I don't like to be inquisitive, but I don't like working in the dark either.
Hopalong Cassidy played by William Boyd in <u>Renegade Trail</u> *(1939)*

There are two kinds of people I don't like: those that claim they know nothing and those that claim they know everything.
Lt. Stafford played by Ettore Manni in <u>The Stranger Returns</u> *(1968)*

LADY

I'm a lady and I'm going to be treated like a lady! The next one of you hoodlums that sets foot in this carriage gets a shot right in the gut!
Emma McGee played by Hope Emerson in Belle Le Grande (1951)

A lady doesn't allow a situation to get beyond her control.
Ivette Rivage played by Lisa Daniels in The Gambler from Natchez (1954)

April: What did you expect lady women to be like?
Dusty: Oh, kind of like the scenery: good to look at but kind of frostbitten.
April Logan played by Madeleine Carroll and Dusty Rivers played by Gary Cooper in North West Mounted Police (1940)

If you want her to act like a lady, you got to treat her like one.
Katie played by Amy Carlson in Peacemakers (2003)

LAND

The land's not much good to you when you're six feet under it.
The Stranger played by Jim Davis in The Badge of Marshal Brennan (1957)

There's only one thing on this earth more important than money, and that's land.
Adarene Clinch played by Mary Ann Edwards in Giant (1956)

Ramona: You speak of the earth as if it were a woman.

Alessandro: Well, isn't it always a woman who gives life?

Ramona played by Loretta Young and Alessandro played by Don Ameche in <u>Ramona</u> *(1936)*

LANGUAGE

Spud: There ain't anybody in the world that can sing like you.

Chiquita: Isn't anybody in the world.

Spud: Ain't that what I said?

Spud Kilton played by Bobby Driscoll and Chiquita McSweeney played by Jane Frazee in <u>The Big Bonanza</u> *(1944)*

I like listening to this Mexican radio station. I don't understand anything but I like the way Spanish sounds.

The Old Man with Radio played by Levon Helm in <u>The Three Burials of Melquiades Estrada</u> *(2005)*

LAST STRAW

I say this is the last straw. I came back from the war, my farm was burned down, my cows were dead. And now my wife has run off with my cousin, Jeb. The son-of-a-bitch! He took my dog!

Loni Packwood played by Joe Stevens in <u>American Outlaws</u> *(2001)*

LAST WORD

Race: [Guns] always have the last word and they always will.

Sheriff: Maybe the loudest, but this [badge] has the last.

Race Crim played by Dale Robertson and Sheriff Tom Davisson played by Rory Calhoun in <u>The Silver Whip</u> *(1953)*

LATER

Later may be too late.

Nugget Clark played by Eddy Waller in <u>Oklahoma Badlands</u> *(1948)*

LAUGHTER

You'd probably crack your face if you laughed out loud.
Constable Alvin Adams played by Andrew Stevens in <u>Death Hunt</u> (1981)

LAW & ORDER

Law and order never came to any community without brave men paying for it
with their lives.
Judge Clayton L. Meade played by Edward LeSaint in <u>Arizona Legion</u> (1939)

I calc'late to keep law an' order in this here town ... if I have to shoot the hull
population.
Judge Haller played by James Marcus in <u>The Iron Horse</u> (1924)

LAWLESSNESS

The town sort of works on a 'live and let live' basis with a touch of 'every man
for himself' thrown in.
The Clerk played by Stephen R. Miller in <u>Broken Trail</u> (2006)

Chip ain't really bad at heart. He's just wild and reckless and sort of
headstrong. It's the lawless condition of the country that's to blame,
encouraging our young men to swing a wide loop.
John Douglas played by Tom Brower in <u>Land Beyond the Law</u> (1937)

You can't stop lawlessness with more lawlessness.
Sheriff Lucky Crandall played by Russell Hayden in <u>A Tornado in the Saddle</u> (1942)

LAWMEN

It is the duty of us peace officers to help people as well as arrest them.
Johnny Nelson played by James Ellison in <u>The Eagle's Brood</u> (1935)

I'm all for law and order, Marshal, but a lawman has got to take the long view.
Sheriff Bartlett played by Walter Sande in <u>Last Train from Gun Hill</u> (1959)

I've seen men like you in every town in the west. You want the law but you want it to walk quiet. You don't want it to put a hole in your pocket.
Marshal Jared Maddox played by Burt Lancaster in <u>Lawman</u> (1971)

The sheriff's dead! Long live the sheriff!
Cuthbert J. Twillie played by W.C. Fields in <u>My Little Chickadee</u> (1940)

I'm a sheriff, not a whole posse!
The Sheriff played by Chubby Johnson in <u>Night Riders of Montana</u> (1951)

Catching small fries always scatters the big fish.
Hopalong Cassidy played by William Boyd in <u>Stagecoach War</u> (1940)

Sheriff: Why let him get away?
Tim: Because if you follow a coyote long enough, he takes you right back to his den.
Sheriff Purdy played by Gordon DeMain and Tim Barrett played by Tim McCoy in <u>The Western Code</u> (1932)

Dan: Why did you let him go for? We had him right in our hands.
Allan: Sometimes you got to use little fish to catch big ones.
Wyoming Dan played by Trevor Bardette and Allan "Rocky" Lane played himself in <u>The Wyoming Bandit</u> (1949)

LAWS

The only law that this country respects is the law of the gun and the rope.
Rawhide Morgan played by Jack Holt in <u>The Arizona Ranger</u> (1948)

There's an old saying in the British Army: the law must always save its face in front of the natives.
Wade Hatton played by Errol Flynn in <u>Dodge City</u> (1939)

Your law blows in the wind. It says what you want it to say.
Ollokot played by Emilio Delgado in <u>I Will Fight No More Forever</u> (1975)

That's the trouble with our laws: they're all so full of loopholes.
Renn Frayne played by Russell Hayden in Knights of the Range (1940)

LAWYERS

I'm not opening any letter from a lawyer on an empty stomach.
John O'Hanlan played by James Stewart in The Cheyenne Social Club (1970)

The last time that bear ate a lawyer, he had the runs for thirty-three days.
Judge Roy Bean played by Paul Newman in The Life and Times of Judge Roy Bean (1972)

Judge: Mr. Calhoun, you don't seem to have counsel.
Ben: I'll handle my own case, your honor.
Judge: You'll handle your own. You have a fool for a client.
Judge Bidelle played by Cliff Hall and Ben Calhoun played by Dale Robertson in Scalplock (1967)

Four suggestions I can leave you: explain nothing; deny everything; demand the proof; don't listen to it.
Swiftwater Tilton played by Adolphe Menjou in Timberjack (1955)

I'm a lawyer, not the law.
Will Blue played by Henry Fonda in Welcome to Hard Times (1967)

This lawyer will be perfect for you. You see, he's the undertaker too.
Josh Huckings played by Lee Roberts in Wild Country (1947)

Windy: I guess maybe it don't show on me, but I started out to be a lawyer.
Charles: A lawyer? Well, I guess looks are kind of deceiving. You look honest.
Windy Gibson played by George "Gabby" Hayes and Charles Alderson played by William "Wild Bill" Elliott in Wyoming (1947)

LEAD

Why, you've seen the time when I was so dern full of lead that I didn't dare go in swimming.
Windy Halliday played by George "Gabby" Hayes in <u>In Old Mexico</u> (1938)

Remember that a slug of lead can catch up with you.
Gene Autry played himself in <u>The Last Round-Up</u> (1947)

Don't shoot! I'm allergic to lead!
Cornelius J. Courtney played by Jimmy Durante in <u>Melody Ranch</u> (1940)

Hot lead isn't on my diet.
Frosty Larson played by Al St. John in <u>Texas Terrors</u> (1940)

LEADERS

It's a pity, isn't it, that those who rule can never be loved?
Wilson played by Robert Mitchum in <u>Bandido</u> (1956)

Like the raven, the eagle flies alone, Sam. Only the wind supports him. That's all he needs. Just fly. Others will follow.
Tiana Rogers played by Devon Ericson in <u>Gone to Texas</u> (1986)

We just need one man to get on a horse and say, 'Charge!' We can do the rest.
Uncle Jimmy played by Jerry Haynes in <u>Gone to Texas</u> (1986)

Not all chiefs are leaders and not all leaders are chiefs.
Kulakinah played by Wes Studi in <u>The Lone Ranger</u> (2003)

A good trail boss always rides at the head of his outfit.
Mary Gordon played by Sheila Mannors/Sheila Bromley in <u>Westward Ho</u> (1935)

LEARNING

The only way to learn some folks is to knock it into their head.
Frank McClosky played by Ray Mayer in The Arizonian (1935)

You got a lot of unlearning to do.
Johnny Wade played by Brian Keith in The Bull of the West (1971)

We better learn to walk before we try to run.
Hopalong Cassidy played by William Boyd in The Frontiersmen (1938)

Nobody is too old to learn.
Mary Wells played by Gloria Grahame in Roughshod (1949)

Right now he's a little long on education and a little short on sense. He's got a lot to learn.
Dr. Daniel Harris, Sr., played by Lewis Stone in Stars in My Crown (1950)

Sometimes you learn things in spite of yourself.
Josh Tanner played by Robert Wagner in White Feather (1955)

LEGACY

You sure did leave an awful big footprint.
Jesse Traven played by Jeff Osterhage in The Shadow Riders (1982)

LEGAL

Being legal don't make it right.
Frank Gifford played by Patrick Lyster in Trigger Fast (1994)

LEGENDS

It's not too bad being a footnote to a legend.
Frank Thayer played by Eion Bailey in And Starring Pancho Villa as Himself (2003)

Publicist: Buffalo Bill writes all of his original things himself.

[Presidential aide whispers in president's ear.]

President: All great men do.

Publicist/Major John Burke played by Kevin McCarthy and President Grover Cleveland played by Pat McCormick in <u>Buffalo Bill and the Indians, or Sitting Bull's History Lesson</u> (1976)

There are certain bold and daring men who are destined never to be forgotten. They die, but memory of them lives on, growing into legend.

Prologue in <u>The Last Bandit</u> (1949)

Legends handed down, they're most likely distorted, exaggerated over the years. But I've always found there's a grain of truth in them somehow.

Texas John Cody played by Forrest Tucker in <u>Timestalkers</u> (1987)

Zorro is a legend and legends never die.

Brad "El Lobo" Dace played by Richard Alexander in <u>Zorro Rides Again</u> (1937)

LESSONS

Leonard: Do they still shoot deserters?

Bronco Billy: Well, it would teach you a lesson if they did!

Leonard James played by Sam Bottoms and Bronco Billy played by Clint Eastwood in <u>Bronco Billy</u> (1980)

No pain, no gain.

Angela played by Rosemary Murphy in <u>Dust</u> (2001)

Sometimes it's necessary to make mistakes before learning a lesson.

The voice of Stormy was that of Barbara Jean Wong in <u>The Man from Button Willow</u> (1965)

Townsman: Have you anything to say [before being hanged]?

Cuthbert: Ah, yes, this is going to be a great lesson to me.

Townsman was uncredited and Cuthbert J. Twillie played by W.C. Fields in <u>My Little Chickadee</u> (1940)

LEVELS

He's just where he always was. It's just that we sank so far beneath him.

Mrs. Decrais played by Kathryn Givney in <u>Count Three and Pray</u> (1955)

LIBERATORS

There had been two liberators. But one of them had turned dictator. It's a habit that liberators often get into, and it tends to confuse the people they've liberated.

Tom Bryan played by Rory Calhoun in <u>The Treasure of Pancho Villa</u> (1955)

LIBERTY

Liberty can never compromise with tyranny or dictatorship.

Connie Faulkner played by Adrian Booth/Lorna Gray in <u>The Gallant Legion</u> (1948)

LIFE

Life is a little thing unless it's one's own.

Pancho Lopez played by Wallace Beery in <u>The Bad Man</u> (1941)

I think maybe life gets its meaning from the way we live up to the choices and commitments that we make.

Sarah Johnson played by Nancy Sorel in <u>Black Fox: Good Men and Bad</u> (1995)

Into every life a little rain must fall.

James Wylie played by Dennis Morgan in <u>Cheyenne</u> (1947)

You're going to wear yourself out if you keep fighting every bump.

Ross McEwen played by Joel McCrea in <u>Four Faces West</u> (1948)

The best parts of life are the little ones all added up.
Amos Russell played by M.C. Gainey in <u>The Last Cowboy</u> *(2003)*

Life is short—shorter for some than others.
Gus McCrea played by Robert Duvall in <u>Lonesome Dove</u> *(1989)*

Do you ever wonder if you've done the right thing with your life?
Mother Superior played by Jean Speegle Howard in <u>Los Locos</u> *(1997)*

You can't turn back the clock.
Kit Banion played by Barbara Stanwyck in <u>The Maverick Queen</u> *(1956)*

How like life the bubble is. It's a beautiful thing. It floats for a little while,
going where it will at the whim of the wind, and then it's gone.
Samuel Clemens played by James Garner in <u>Roughing It</u> *(2002)*

Life is just like a bank. You can't take out any more than you put in.
Tom Lawson played by Tom Mix in <u>Rustlers' Roundup</u> *(1933)*

LIFE & DEATH

Too bad you have to die before you have lived.
Pancho Lopez played by Wallace Beery in <u>The Bad Man</u> *(1941)*

I just want to get out of this life alive.
Linc played by Gabriel Casseus in <u>Brothers in Arms</u> *(2005)*

Though I am dead, the grass will grow, the sun will shine, the stream will flow.
Yellow Hand played by Anthony Quinn, saying Indian prayer in <u>Buffalo Bill</u> *(1944)*

Don't think of it as the end of your life; think of it as the beginning of your death.
Captain Starrett played by Bo Svenson in <u>Cheyenne</u> *(1996)*

In life we are ever close to death.
Don Luana played by Anthony Warde in <u>Don Ricardo Returns</u> (1946)

Live your own life because you die your own death.
Angela played by Rosemary Murphy in <u>Dust</u> (2001)

You're just walking around to save funeral expenses.
Charlotta played by Valerie Perrine in <u>The Electric Horseman</u> (1979)

There's a mother, a midwife, maybe a doctor when a man is born. But you schedule his death, and you put it on a calendar, and people will come from all over the territory just to see the spectacle.
Brady Hawkes played by Kenny Rogers in <u>Gambler V: Playing for Keeps</u> (1994)

He'd die for you, but he's not going to live his life for you.
Leslie Lynnton Benedict played by Elizabeth Taylor in <u>Giant</u> (1956)

It ain't how they bring you in or carry you out that matters. It's what you do while you're here that they remember you by.
Elias Hobbes played by Wallace Ford in <u>The Great Jesse James Raid</u> (1953)

Killing one Indian wouldn't do any good. Letting one live might.
Jim Bridger played by Dennis Morgan in <u>The Gun That Won the West</u> (1955)

Nobody gets out of life alive.
Hud Bannon played by Paul Newman in <u>Hud</u> (1963)

To live one must first die.
John W. Gamble played by Richard Boone in <u>Kangaroo</u> (1952)

Nothing can live unless something dies.
Gay Langland played by Clark Gable in <u>The Misfits</u> (1961)

My mother always says it is better to live poor than to die rich.
Chito Rafferty played by Richard Martin in <u>Nevada</u> (1944)

You think about death too much. You need to start thinking about what's still alive.
Lana played by Salli Richardson in <u>Posse</u> (1993)

One time a wise man said, 'Though I can see that tomorrow would end, I go plant in the earth an apple sapling today.'
Professor Hampel played by Heinz Erhardt in <u>Rampage at Apache Wells</u> (1965)

Sometimes it is better to die like a man than to live like a coward.
Don Alejandro de la Vega played by George J. Lewis in <u>The Sign of Zorro</u> (1960)

LIFE INSURANCE
Nobody likes to pay too much for life insurance.
Joe Faringo played by Akim Tamiroff in <u>Relentless</u> (1948)

LIFE STORY
Why don't you tell me the story of your life. Just skip everything but the last few minutes.
Luke Matthews played by James Coburn in <u>Bite the Bullet</u> (1975)

LIGHTNING ROD
You are a damn lightning rod! I've never known anybody at the center of so many storms!
President Andrew Jackson played by G.D. Spradlin in <u>Gone to Texas</u> (1986)

LIKENESS
We're all cut from the same cloth.
Lon Cordeen played by Gordon Scott in <u>The Tramplers</u> (1966)

LINES
There's a line. You cross it, you have to pay the penalty.
Marshal Jim Cogan played by Kent Taylor in <u>The Broken Land</u> (1962)

A man's got to draw the line someplace if he's going to go on living with himself.
Morley Chase played by Ray Teal in <u>Decision at Sundown</u> (1957)

LISTENING

Anybody can talk. How do you get folks to listen?
Lissy played by Joanne Woodward in <u>Count Three and Pray</u> (1955)

LONE RIDER

A lone rider does not always mean a problem.
Mrs. Preble played by May Heatherly in <u>Outlaw Justice</u> (1999)

LONELINESS

You don't like loneliness and yet you invite it. Did anyone ever tell you that loneliness is ninety-five percent fear?
Jeannie played by Coleen Gray in <u>The Black Whip</u> (1956)

You can feel lonely anywhere. It isn't the place that makes you lonely.
Dell McGuire played by Maureen O'Hara in <u>Kangaroo</u> (1952)

If I'm going to be alone, I want to be by myself.
Roslyn Taber played by Marilyn Monroe in <u>The Misfits</u> (1961)

I've been alone all my life. Only most of the time, people are around. So on my day off, I go right away from them. On my day off, I get to be alone without them.
Sally Crane played by Fintan Meyler in <u>Showdown at Boot Hill</u> (1958)

A man is only lonely when he depends on other people.
Mike McComb played by Errol Flynn in <u>Silver River</u> (1948)

LOSERS

You're a fourth-rate act in a third-rate show.
Brittany played by April Telek in <u>Dead Man's Gun</u> (1997)

Losers always complain. It's a cross the men of talent must bear.
Fairweather played by Frank Faylen in <u>The Lone Gun</u> *(1954)*

LOSING

I don't mind losing. I just like to have a run for my money.
Tully Crow played by Lee Marvin in <u>The Comancheros</u> *(1961)*

I lost but I'm not a loser.
Jumbo Means played by Raymond Burr in <u>Great Day in the Morning</u> *(1956)*

I am not the only soldier who served in a losing cause, and you are not the only woman to lose a child.
Cable played by Tom Selleck in <u>Last Stand at Saber River</u> *(1997)*

LOST

Well, you know, maybe a compass would have been a wise purchase instead of the four pounds of tortilla chips you bought.
Phil Berquist played by Daniel Stern in <u>City Slickers II: The Legend of Curly's Gold</u> *(1994)*

Celia: Haven't you ever lost anything, Mr. Davis?
Davis: Yes, ma'am, but I learned not to look back.
Celia Gray played by Virginia Mayo and Gar Davis played by Clint Walker in <u>Fort Dobbs</u> *(1958)*

There are a lot of lost souls out there. And without a little help, not many ever find themselves.
Joshua played by Leon Coffee in <u>Jericho</u> *(2000)*

LOST & FOUND

You look as though you lost a dollar and found a dime.
Wade Hatton played by Errol Flynn in <u>Dodge City</u> *(1939)*

I don't want to know where he ain't. I want to know where he is.
Bert Lynn played by James Gleason in <u>The Story of Will Rogers</u> (1952)

LOVE

Do you know what water is to fire? That's what sense is to love.
Sol Levy played by David Opatoshu in <u>Cimarron</u> (1960)

Greater Love Hath No Man Than This: That A Man Lay Down His Life For His Friends.
Tombstone Inscription in <u>Colorado Sunset</u> (1939)

Love is so hard to find and so easy to lose.
Claire Gordon played by Mae Clarke in <u>Flaming Gold</u> (1933)

Love has got to be a fair game. It isn't Solitaire either. Two have got to play it to make it worthwhile.
Ramirez played by Nelson Eddy in <u>The Girl of the Golden West</u> (1938)

If you love a man, he can do everything wrong.
Bess Banner played by Barbara Britton in <u>Gunfighters</u> (1947)

Aunt Carrie: Do you believe in love at first sight?
Jeff: I reckon I do. But I don't see so well.
Aunt Carrie Burton played by Fay Holden and Jeff Carter played by Eddie Acuff in <u>Guns of the Pecos</u> (1937)

Love is something one must share.
Paviva played by Lisa Montell in <u>The Lone Ranger and the Lost City of Gold</u> (1958)

Hatred stirs up discontent, but love covers over all wrong.
Daniel Fowler played by Alec Medlock, paraphrasing Proverb 10, Verse 12, of the Bible, in <u>The Long Ride Home</u> (2003)

You know, sometimes love isn't fireworks. Sometimes love just comes softly.
Sarah Graham played by Theresa Russell in <u>Love Comes Softly</u> (2003)

I might be leaving but my love is staying here with you.
Marty Claridge played by Katherine Heigl in <u>Love Comes Softly</u> (2003)

It's no harder to love a rich man than a poor one.
Isobelle McKenzie played by Helen Cates in <u>A Mother's Gift</u> (1995)

If you're in love with someone, you don't make conditions.
Ann Dennison played by Peggie Castle in <u>Overland Pacific</u> (1954)

I've seen love take seed in rockier ground than this. But sometimes it takes mighty tender cultivation.
Parson Jackson played by Tom Tully in <u>Rachel and the Stranger</u> (1948)

A famous poet once said: 'The embers of love may smolder, but they never die.'
Janie Pritchard played by Jane Withers in <u>Shooting High</u> (1940)

'Then comes the lover, sighing like a furnace.'
Riley played by J.M. Kerrigan, quoting Shakespeare, in <u>The Silver Whip</u> (1953)

Very often we destroy the ones nearest to our hearts. And the irony of it is, we destroy them with our love, with our forbearance, exaggerating their frail and little virtues and blinding ourselves to their very obvious vices.
Dr. Julia Winslow Garth played by Greer Garson in <u>Strange Lady in Town</u> (1955)

It's always nice to fall in love with someone you like.
Mabel King played by Joan Davis in <u>The Traveling Saleswoman</u> (1950)

Falling in love without heartaches is just like trying to eat crackers without leaving a crumb.
Daisy played by Lillian Yarbo in <u>Wild Bill Hickok Rides</u> (1942)

LOVE LETTER

My Dearest Lily: I take pen in hand to write you for this very last time. I wish to tell you that although I have never seen you, or heard the sound of your voice, I have carried you with me in my heart always. Your presence on this earth has given me strength and dignity becoming a gentleman; it helps me to drive away the cold on a long and lonely night. I wish to say, lastly, it has been an honor to adore you. God willing, sometime in this life, or afterwards, I may yet stand in your light and declare myself forever and ever your ardent admirer and champion. Judge Roy Bean.

Letter from Judge Roy Bean, played by Paul Newman, to Lily Langtry, played by Ava Gardner, in The Life and Times of Judge Roy Bean *(1972)*

LOYALTY

I don't think you should criticize the company, particularly when you're eating at their plate.

Harry Banning played by Rollo Lloyd in Flaming Gold *(1933)*

A man only owes one loyalty—to himself.

Corporal Bodine played by Kenneth Tobey in 40 Guns to Apache Pass *(1967)*

A man likes to know his woman will back him when he's down.

Grant McLaine played by James Stewart in Night Passage *(1957)*

You take my money, you wear my brand.

Hawk played by Richard Jordan in Rooster Cogburn *(1975)*

When you side with a man, that's it.

The Virginian played by Bill Pullman in The Virginian *(1999)*

LUCK

Don't frown on luck, my friend, or she will frown on you.

The Drunk was uncredited in Gore Vidal's Billy the Kid *(1989)*

Well, it's better your toes [shot off] than your fingers. I think that's kind of lucky.
Ned played by Tim Scott in <u>Kid Vengeance</u> (1977)

I don't win because I'm lucky.
John Herod played by Gene Hackman in <u>The Quick and the Dead</u> (1995)

You're not bad luck. You've just had bad luck is all.
Jake Roedel played by Tobey Maguire in <u>Ride With the Devil</u> (1999)

I've always been a man that made his own luck.
Harry Wringle played by Willis Bouchey in <u>Two Rode Together</u> (1961)

LYING

The trouble with a liar is, he can't remember what he said.
The Judge played by Bruce Dern in <u>All the Pretty Horses</u> (2000)

Every prairie hole is a gold mine, every molehill is a mountain, every creek is a river, and everybody you meet is a liar.
Jack Parker played by Dabney Coleman in <u>Bite the Bullet</u> (1975)

I thought I had a good reason for lying to you. But I guess lies, even for good reasons, never seem to turn out right.
Mary Justin played by Lois Nettleton in <u>The Bull of the West</u> (1971)

I did not lie! I did not tell the truth. But I did not lie.
Sacajawea played by Donna Reed in <u>The Far Horizons</u> (1955)

It is usually a lie that keeps people apart.
Jim Killian played by Glenn Ford in <u>Heaven with a Gun</u> (1969)

A good liar never puts anything in print.
Scott Yager played by Eddie Dew in <u>Red River Robin Hood</u> (1943)

MAIL

Mail from anywhere is a comfort as long as it's not addressed from some jail or prison.
Butch Cassidy played by Scott Paulin in <u>Gambler V: Playing for Keeps</u> (1994)

MANHOOD

Prairie Flower: You must eat if you want to grow to manhood.
White Bull: It is not food that keeps me from becoming a man.
Prairie Flower played by Joy Page and White Bull played by Sal Mineo in <u>Tonka</u> (1958)

MANNERS

It's not very good manners telling a lady she smells.
Johnny Cobb played by James Stewart in <u>Firecreek</u> (1968)

What do I need manners for? I already got me a wife.
Adam Pontipee played by Howard Keel in <u>Seven Brides for Seven Brothers</u> (1954)

It's bad manners to shoot in a church.
Etta Place played by Katharine Ross in <u>Wanted: The Sundance Woman</u> (1976)

MARKSMANSHIP

Here in the West, the cemeteries are full of people who thought they were good shots.
Cole Harvey played by Robert Woods in <u>The Belle Starr Story</u> *(1967)*

He did it! He missed the barn!
Clay Boone played by Michael Callan in <u>Cat Ballou</u> *(1965)*

You couldn't hit water if you fell out of a damn canoe!
Bear played by Norman Brown in <u>The Doe Boy</u> *(2001)*

You couldn't hit the bottom of a toilet with a turd!
Bear played by Norman Brown in <u>The Doe Boy</u> *(2001)*

While he was shooting fast, I was aiming carefully.
Bill Schell played by Don DeFore in <u>Ramrod</u> *(1947)*

MARRIAGE

As far as our marriage goes, we could do it over the phone.
Jack Twist played by Jake Gyllenhaal in <u>Brokeback Mountain</u> *(2005)*

I went with an old gal for quite a while. We was laying in bed one morning and suddenly she sprung it on me. She said, 'Dodger, don't you think it's about time that we was getting hitched?' And I said, 'Well, do you suppose anybody would have us?'
Dodger played by Richard Farnsworth in <u>Comes a Horseman</u> *(1978)*

There's nothing like a happy marriage to keep a woman looking beautiful.
Sheriff O'Hea played by Edgar Buchanan in <u>Coroner Creek</u> *(1948)*

Mac: I can afford to get married.
Curly: I can afford not to.
Mac played by Richard Reeves and Curly Adams played by George Wallace in <u>Destry</u> *(1954)*

If you can get your father's consent, we'll get married if I can get my wife's consent.
S. Quentin Quale played by Groucho Marx in Go West (1940)

Ruth: You're marrying me for my cooking!
Ben: Oh, absolutely! What are you marrying me for?
Ruth Granger played by Maggie Hayes and Ben Cutler played by Fred MacMurray in Good Day for a Hanging (1958)

Cattle Kate: I wouldn't marry a low-life hyena like you if you were the last man on earth.
Shorty: Well, if I was the last man on earth maybe I wouldn't ask you.
Mrs. "Cattle Kate" Turner played by Irene Franklin and Deputy "Shorty" Long played by Frank Orth in Land Beyond the Law (1937)

Now while I realize that Jesus was born in a stable, I will not allow my daughter to marry a boy who lives in one.
Josiah Peale played by Paul Le Mat in Lonesome Dove: Tales of the Plains (1992)

Marriage was an easy way for us to get what we both wanted.
Claire McLeod played by Tammy McIntosh in McLeod's Daughters (1995)

The best marriages aren't necessarily the ones that start in love, Abby. Marriages that start with mutual respect and affection, now they often end in love.
William "Will" Deal played by Adrian Pasdar (in a letter to girl) in A Mother's Gift (1995)

I wanted to marry her when I saw the moonlight shinning on the barrel of her father's shotgun.
Ali Hakim played by Eddie Albert in Oklahoma! (1955)

In marriage, sometimes it's better to think back to the beginning.
Pancho Villa played by Telly Savalas in Pancho Villa (1972)

The glory of a good marriage don't come at the beginning. It comes later on. It's hard work.
Judge Tolliver played by Edgar Buchanan in <u>Ride the High Country</u> (1962)

Kathy: We're going to be married the minute we go to Boston.
Major: What's that old saw about 'married in haste, we may repent at leisure'?
Kathy played by Mary Murphy and Major Robert "Bob" Parrish played by Dale Robertson in <u>Sitting Bull</u> (1954)

Shut up! You can't talk like that to me until after we're married!
Junior Potter played by Bob Hope in <u>Son of Paleface</u> (1952)

Deceipt is not a good foundation for marriage.
Jackson "Sugarfoot" Redan played by Randolph Scott in <u>Sugarfoot</u> (1951)

I doubt if advice about marriage is much good to anyone.
Jackson "Sugarfoot" Redan played by Randolph Scott in <u>Sugarfoot</u> (1951)

MASKED RIDER

A masked rider can be a very dangerous menace in a law-abiding community.
Collins played by Ted Adams in <u>Phantom Rancher</u> (1940)

MEDICINE

Until your dying day, you are going to thank me for selling you that bottle of remedy.
Professor Wentworth played by Earle Hodgins in <u>Home on the Prairie</u> (1939)

MEDICINE SHOW

Oh, here's that letter I was looking for. This man here, he says, 'For years,' he says, 'I suffered from insomnia. I had a bad case of insomnia. But,' he says, 'after taking only one bottle,' you notice they say just one bottle, neighbor, just one bottle, that after taking one bottle of Zerbo Indian Remedy, 'my insomnia is completely cured!' Isn't that nice? He says, 'I lay awake nights thinking of how I used to suffer from it.'
Doc Rufus Tate/Bates played by Earle Hodgins in <u>Santa Fe Marshal</u> (1940)

MEETING

If we're going to have a meeting, it better come to more than just poking holes in the air with your finger.
Ernie Wright played by Leonard Strong in <u>Shane</u> *(1953)*

MEMORIES

But soon the memories will grow dim, as memories should. And there will be others to take their place. May they be happy ones for you.
Sacajawea played by Donna Reed in <u>The Far Horizons</u> *(1955)*

Memory holds on to things.
Govern Sturges played by John Lund in <u>Five Guns West</u> *(1955)*

All I got left to hang on to are a few memories.
Alec Waggoman played by Donald Crisp in <u>The Man from Laramie</u> *(1955)*

I really love that song, you know that, Jeff. It reminds me of my fifth wife.
Gimme Cap played by Dub Taylor in <u>My Heroes Have Always Been Cowboys</u> *(1991)*

MEN

A man can't help the way he is.
Logan Cates played by Rory Calhoun in <u>Apache Territory</u> *(1958)*

I believe a man is as big as what he's seeking.
Reno Smith played by Robert Ryan in <u>Bad Day at Black Rock</u> *(1955)*

Not all males are men.
Innocencio Ortega played by Gilbert Roland in <u>Three Violent People</u> *(1956)*

MEN & WOMEN

Do you undress every woman you meet?
Charity Warwick played by Victoria Shaw in <u>Alvarez Kelly</u> *(1966)*

Once in awhile, the gentle touch of a woman helps soothe the savage beast within a man.
Winston Patrick Culler played by Wilford Brimley in <u>Blood River</u> (1991)

One rule stands fast the world over, ma'am. Whether prince or pauper, a man's only as good as the woman that stands beside him.
Bill Foster played by Drake Smith in <u>Cattle Queen</u> (1951)

A man sees things so differently from a woman.
Mary Baker played by Iris Meredith in <u>The Cowboy Star</u> (1936)

Men have to fight and women have to cry.
Max played by Reni Santoni in <u>Guns of the Magnificent Seven</u> (1969)

Sometimes all it takes for a man to find himself is for some woman to inspire him.
Carolina Cotton played herself in <u>Hoedown</u> (1950)

I never saw a man yet that was so smart that some woman couldn't make a fool out of him.
Lucky Jenkins played by Russell Hayden in <u>In Old Mexico</u> (1938)

Belle: How many women have you visited before you come to see me?
Cole: This is my first stop.
Belle Shirley Starr played by Pamela Reed and Cole Younger played by David Carradine in <u>The Long Riders</u> (1980)

Let's put it this way: where there are two men and one girl on top of a mountain, it's trouble.
Sam McCord played by John Wayne in <u>North to Alaska</u> (1960)

That's the way with you men: a new flame always burns the brightest.
Jen Larrabee played by Gail Davis in <u>On Top of Old Smoky</u> (1953)

I like you better when you're more bashful and not so boastful.
Eleanor played by Lucile Browne in <u>Rainbow Valley</u> (1935)

Why do women always want to change a man?
Rooster Cogburn played by John Wayne in <u>Rooster Cogburn</u> (1975)

Why do women insist on loving men for what they want them to be instead of what they are?
Brice Chamberlain played by Melvyn Douglas in <u>The Sea of Grass</u> (1947)

One thing I can't stand is a man that forces himself on a girl who wouldn't be caught dead with him.
Tom Elder played by Dean Martin in <u>The Sons of Katie Elder</u> (1965)

MIDDLE AGE

Do you ever reach a point in your life when you say to yourself: 'This is the best I'm ever going to look, the best I'm ever going to feel, the best I'm ever going to do, and it ain't that great.'
Mitch Robbins played by Billy Crystal in <u>City Slickers</u> (1991)

MIND

The mind is its own place, and of itself, can make a hell of heaven, a heaven of hell.
Brian Athlone played by Don Wycherley in <u>One Man's Hero</u> (1999)

I was hoping your mind had grown up with the rest of you.
Zoe Fontaine played by Colleen Miller in <u>The Rawhide Years</u> (1956)

MIRACLE

Miracles don't come in pairs.
Doc Ridgeway played by Gus Schilling in <u>Run for Cover</u> (1955)

MISDEEDS

Man with his misdeeds kindles his own hellfire!
Caption in <u>Hellfire</u> *(1949)*

MISERY

Misery loves company, I guess.
Dave Mosely played by Lyle Bettger in <u>Showdown at Abilene</u> *(1956)*

MISTAKES

When I take the count, it will be for my own mistakes.
Dave Nash played by Joel McCrea in <u>Ramrod</u> *(1947)*

You make one mistake, that's your fault. You make another mistake, that's my fault.
Milton Keefe played by Willard Robertson in <u>The Texas Bad Man</u> *(1932)*

I've lost all my patience with a man that sticks by his mistakes when he's been cleaned out by them.
Beech Carter played by Larry Wilcox in <u>Trail of Danger</u> *(1977)*

We all make our mistakes. The lesson is in the learning from them.
Eugene Lawson played by Ernest Borgnine in <u>The Trail to Hope Rose</u> *(2004)*

MOBS

Take away the leader from the mob, and there is no mob.
Fredo Brios played by John Dehner in <u>California Conquest</u> *(1952)*

If a mob does it, nobody gets any blame.
Johnny Reno played by Dana Andrews in <u>Johnny Reno</u> *(1966)*

Crowds don't lynch people. That was a mob.
Matt Dow played by James Cagney in <u>Run for Cover</u> *(1955)*

MODESTY

Sam: Come on out [of the water], pronto.

Phoebe: Well, I can't. I haven't any clothes on!

Sam: Well, shut your eyes.

Sam Hollis played by Dean Martin and Phoebe Ann Naylor played by Rosemary Forsyth in Texas Across the River (1966)

MONEY

Water is water, and fire is fire; where money is concerned, every man is a liar.

Honest Plush Brannon played by Wallace Beery in Barbary Coast Gent (1944)

Never use money to measure wealth.

Print Ritter played by Robert Duvall in Broken Trail (2006)

Grandma used to say having money can't bring happiness. But it sure is a most pleasant way of being miserable.

Stretch Barnes/Smoky Callaway played by Howard Keel in Callaway Went Thataway (1951)

It seems to me like you're struggling your way past a dollar just to grub after a dime.

Lincoln "Linc" Costain played by James Garner in The Castaway Cowboy (1974)

When I first came out to this country, you could get a wife, a team of horses, and a quart of whiskey for a dollar. Of course, it wasn't very good whiskey.

Judge Harmon played by Jed Prouty in Go West, Young Lady (1941)

Money is a great power.

Ethan Hoyt played by Joel McCrea in The Great Man's Lady (1942)

Nothing don't go very far!

Frank Clemens played by Jack Elam in Hannie Caulder (1971)

Isn't it surprising how romantic women can get about money?
Jeff McCloud played by Robert Mitchum in <u>The Lusty Men</u> (1952)

Money splits better two ways instead of three.
Ben Vandergroat played by Robert Ryan in <u>The Naked Spur</u> (1953)

Half of it I spent on whiskey and women, and the other half I wasted.
Yaqui Joe played by Burt Reynolds in <u>100 Rifles</u> (1969)

There's no sense throwing good money after bad.
Dolan played by George Peppard in <u>Rough Night in Jericho</u> (1967)

The love of money is the root of all evil.
Nehemiah Mather played by James Westerfield in <u>Scalplock</u> (1967)

You got to spend money to make money.
Harry Farrel played by Warren William in <u>Wild Bill Hickok Rides</u> (1942)

MONUMENTS
Every town should have a monument to its past.
Robert Emerson played by Warner Anderson in <u>The Last Posse</u> (1953)

MORALS
These fire and brimstone fools are ruining the natural way people live, trying to impose their morals on others, forcing lawmakers to pass laws that everybody breaks when the sun goes down.
Miss Rosalee played by Sheryl Lee Ralph in <u>The Gambler Returns: The Luck of the Draw</u> (1991)

MORNINGS
Mornings are a great invention. Every one of them is a beginning of a new day.
Ben Lear played by Pat O'Brien in <u>Flaming Gold</u> (1933)

There's nothing that I hate more than people who get up early in the morning singing and whistling and dispensing joy and laughter.
G. Gatsby (Shakespear) Holmes played by Joe Caits in Hollywood Cowboy *(1937)*

They always start out fine until you wake up and get out of bed.
Calem Ware played by Randolph Scott in A Lawless Street *(1955)*

This is the only time of the day I feel free.
Fan played by Rosanna Schiaffino in The Man Called Noon *(1973)*

MORTGAGE

Gloria: You're born, you get married, you pay taxes, and die.
Pappy: There's just one thing you forgot, ma'am. That's getting the mortgage. That comes between the taxes and dying.
Gloria Baxter played by Renee Godfrey and Pappy played by Roscoe Ates in Down Missouri Way *(1946)*

MOTHERS

When my children need a shelter from the storm on some dark night, you'll find me where I always was: on the porch of our home with a lantern in my hand.
Margaret "Abby" Deal played by Nancy McKeon in A Mother's Gift *(1995)*

Mother: By the way, you're getting married.
Son: I am? Well, congratulations to me! Anyone I know?
Mother: Of course! What kind of mother do you think I am?
The Mother/Matilda Kingsley played by Agnes Moorehead and the Son/Wade Kingsley, Jr., played by Jerry Lewis in Pardners *(1956)*

One mother is very much like another.
Jack Bull Chiles played by Skett Ulrich in Ride With the Devil *(1999)*

Even killers and gunmen have mothers.
Clay Blaisdell played by Henry Fonda in Warlock *(1959)*

MOTIVES

You're after power. I'm after money.
Zero Quick played by Edward Howard in The Scarlet Horseman (1946)

MOUTH

Your mouth is your worst enemy once you start to talk with it.
Lincoln "Linc" Corey played by Jim Davis in California Passage (1950)

The bigger the mouth, the smarter you look when you keep it closed.
Brady Hawkes played by Kenny Rogers in The Gambler: The Adventure Continues (1983)

Why don't you give your mouth the rest of the day off?
Sam Longwood played by Lee Marvin in The Great Scout and Cathouse Thursday (1976)

You ought to shut your mouth. Your mind is hanging out!
Tom Early, Jr., played by Steve Rowland in Gun Glory (1957)

You can't open your mouth without getting your foot in it, can you?
Billy Carson played by Buster Crabbe in Oath of Vengeance (1944)

It seems like my tongue just gallops away with my brain sometimes.
Mary played by Hope Landin in Sugarfoot (1951)

MOVING ON

We have to say goodbye to some things. They was good things in their time.
But the way I see it, their time wore out for us.
Big Eli Wakefield played by Burt Lancaster in The Kentuckian (1955)

MUD

Mud don't care who it splashes.
Ed Yates played by John Larch in Man in the Shadow (1957)

MURDER

It's a sad day when murder is committed in the name of justice.
The Preacher played by J. Don Ferguson in <u>The Long Riders</u> (1980)

'For murder, though it have no tongue, will speak with most miraculous organ.'
Swiftwater Tilton played by Adolphe Menjou, quoting Shakespeare, in <u>Timberjack</u> (1955)

MUSIC

One man's noise is another man's music.
Winston Patrick Culler played by Wilford Brimley in <u>Blood River</u> (1991)

Music has got power.
Doc Meadowlark played by Paul Hurst in <u>Outcasts of the Trail</u> (1949)

I never did know a bad man to have any music in him.
Uncle Shiloh Clegg played by Charles Kemper in <u>Wagonmaster</u> (1950)

MUSTACHE

Never trust a man with a fancy mustache.
Netty Booth played by Karen Valentine in <u>Go West, Young Girl</u> (1978)

NAMES

A man's got to have a name that he can be proud of.
Nat Love played by Ernie Hudson in <u>The Cherokee Kid</u> (1996)

Dusty: My name is Dusty Rivers.
April: A dusty river? Isn't that a contradiction?
Dusty: Why, I expect you've never been to Texas.
*Dusty Rivers played by Gary Cooper and April Logan played by Madeleine Carroll
in <u>North West Mounted Police</u> (1940)*

George: My wife, Geneiva, and me would be proud to have you for supper, Mr.
Shaughnessy.
Tom: 'Tom,' please. I haven't done anything to earn 'mister.'

George: I think you got that backwards.
Now you haven't done anything to
earn 'Tom.'
*George Carpenter played by Michael
White and Tom Shaughnessy played by
Matthew Settle in <u>Shaughnessy</u> (1996)*

I guess it takes more than my having
your name to make me respectable.
*Rose Sharon played by Nancy Kovack in
<u>The Wild Westerners</u> (1962)*

NATION

The claim of the defendants may be true—that gold is the blood of the nation. But the earth is its heart and soul.

The Judge played by Henry O'Neill in <u>Gold Is Where You Find It</u> *(1938)*

NATURE

Sometimes even when smart beaver cut down tree, tree fall on beaver.

Natayo Smith played by Thomas Gomez in <u>Pony Soldier</u> *(1952)*

Atterbury: One minute a guy freezes and another minute he fries.

Braun: Nature is very generous to California.

Dr. "Nuke" Atterbury played by Spencer Charters and Dr. Braun played by Charles Coburn in <u>Three Faces West</u> *(1940)*

NEEDS

If you got nothin', you don't need nothin'.

Ennis Del Mar played by Heath Ledger in <u>Brokeback Mountain</u> *(2005)*

A man needs what he likes.

Ben Vandergroat played by Robert Ryan in <u>The Naked Spur</u> *(1953)*

NEGOTIATION

Why ask for a little when you can get a lot?

Pop Jordan played by George Lloyd in <u>Under California Stars</u> *(1948)*

NEIGHBORS

Neighbors are gonna have to start learning to live together.

Whipple Mondier played by John Ashley, commenting on burying Confederate soldier near grave of Union soldier, in <u>Smoke in the Wind</u> *(1975)*

NERVES

You got more nerve than a bad tooth.

Bridie played by Isabella Hofmann in <u>Independence</u> *(1987)*

That's the trouble with them skinny fellows, though: their nerves are so close to the surface.
Smiley Burnette played himself in Last of the Pony Riders *(1953)*

NEVADA

The slogan of Nevada is 'anything goes.' But don't complain if it went.
Isabelle Steers played by Thelma Ritter in The Misfits *(1961)*

NEVER

Never say never. Say never about something and life will spit it right back at you.
Dora DuFran played by Melanie Griffith in Buffalo Girls *(1995)*

Never is a long time.
Yancey Cravat played by Richard Dix in Cimarron *(1931)*

NEWS

Bad news travels fast.
Jesse Williams played by Stanley Andrews in The Dead Don't Dream *(1948)*

No news is good news.
Vic Rodell played by Stephen McNally in Hell's Crossroads *(1957)*

NEWSPAPERS

A newspaper is the mother's milk of an infant town.
Jason played by Alan Shearman in Black Fox: Good Men and Bad *(1995)*

I still believe the printed word is stronger than guns.
Ned Britt played by Randolph Scott in Fort Worth *(1951)*

Why do they always blame the press for the ills of the world?
Sterling Mott played by Sandy McPeak in Independence *(1987)*

You can't believe all you read in the paper.
Maurine McClune played by Peggy Moran in <u>Rhythm of the Saddle</u> (1938)

NICE

I have always depended on people being nicer than me. And I have never in my life been disappointed.
Esteban played by Ron Leibman in <u>Zorro, the Gay Blade</u> (1981)

NICHE

Everybody has got to be somewhere.
Crecencio played by Luis Avalos in <u>Lone Justice</u> (1994)

A man has to get out and find a place for himself.
Jess Harker played by Robert Wagner in <u>The Silver Whip</u> (1953)

NIGHT

There ain't nothing as lonely as the night.
Dobie played by Richard Rust in <u>Comanche Station</u> (1960)

The night always changes things somehow. Everything seems soft, gentle. It shuts out other things—problems.
Fay Hollister played by Frances Dee in <u>Four Faces West</u> (1948)

NURSES

I know what I'm doing. I ought to. I nursed two husbands to a comfortable grave.
Auntie Mack played by Isabel Withers in <u>Law Men</u> (1944)

OBLIGATIONS

You feel obligations that most men could never bear.

Amy Kane played by Katherine Cannon in <u>High Noon, Part II: The Return of Will Kane</u> (1980)

OBSTACLES

If you run into obstacles, hop 'em. Hop right over 'em!

John Barrabee played by Thurston Hall in <u>Song of Nevada</u> (1944)

OLD-FASHIONED

I guess I'm old-fashioned or just plain old. It's hard to tell at my age.

The Newspaper Editor was uncredited in <u>Vengeance</u> (1968)

OMEN

It's a bad sign, Melody, when the first fella you meet in a town is some kind of hobgoblin.

George Fury played by William Demarest in <u>Along Came Jones</u> (1945)

I knew I never should be a lawman. The first time I pinned this badge on me, I stuck myself.

Sheriff John Mayfield played by Phil Brown in <u>Land Raiders</u> (1969)

OPEN MINDEDNESS

For once, try and act like you don't think things always have to be your way or the highway.
Amos Russell played by M.C. Gainey in The Last Cowboy (2003)

Keep your mind and your heart open.
Jack Beauregard played by Henry Fonda in My Name Is Nobody (1973)

OPINIONS

It's a very narrow-minded person who can't change an opinion.
Jessie Arnold played by Jeff Donnell in Stagecoach Kid (1949)

OPPONENTS

The bigger the tree, the louder the crash.
Jet Cosgrave played by John Derek in The Outcast (1954)

OPPORTUNITY

Nothing is done until it is said and done. And the good Lord always opens a window when He shuts a door.
Devin O'Neil played by Clive Owen in Class of '61 (1993)

There's always a door, Ebenezer, if you choose to open it.
Ghost of Christmas Past played by Michelle Thrush in Ebenezer (1997)

Once or twice in life, if you're really lucky, you get the chance to do something bigger and braver than you think you can.
Amos Russell played by M.C. Gainey in The Last Cowboy (2003)

When a fox is asleep, nothing falls into his mouth.
Frank "Blackie" Marshall played by James Craig in Northwest Rangers (1942)

Tomorrow is always another day. You never can tell just what will happen.
Hopalong Cassidy played by William Boyd in Partners of the Plains (1938)

OPTIMISM

Maybe instead of having ourselves an insolvable problem, what we have is a solution to a lot of other trouble.
Colonel Claude Brackenby played by Melvyn Douglas in Advance to the Rear (1964)

We are as down, broke and defeated as we're ever going to be! And we're on our way back starting right now!
Sierra Nevada Jones played by Barbara Stanwyck in Cattle Queen of Montana (1954)

Let's not be too downcast. Perhaps there is still a ray of sunshine.
Judge Worthington played by Ferris Taylor in Mountain Rhythm (1939)

It's always the darkest before the dawn.
Prunella Judson played by ZaSu Pitts in Ruggles of Red Gap (1935)

That's what I like about you. You could be hanging by your fingers from a cliff and you'd call it 'climbing a mountain.'
Alfie played by Denver Pyle in Welcome to Hard Times (1967)

ORATORS

Georgia is a real orator. She's got all the right bull and bravado.
Sarah McClure played by Dana Delany in True Women (1997)

ORDER

The world has lost its center.
Dog Star played by Gil Birmingham in Into the West (2005)

ORDERS

If you want to give orders, join the Army!
Captain Bill North played by Brian Keith in Arrowhead (1953)

PAIN

If no pain, nothing is born. Even seed burst to make grass.
Batise played by Jean Gascon in <u>A Man Called Horse</u> *(1970)*

Sometimes it helps to share your pain.
Jesse Dalton played by Ben Johnson in <u>My Heroes Have Always Been Cowboys</u> *(1991)*

PASSION

Passion is like a horse. It doesn't diminish just because you harness it. It just takes you where you want to go.
Kulakinah played by Wes Studi in <u>The Lone Ranger</u> *(2003)*

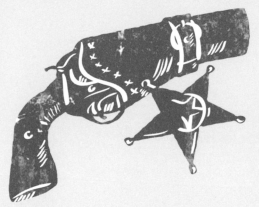

Our passions are like fire and water—good servants but poor masters.
Prologue in <u>Lust in the Dust</u> *(1985)*

I believe that a man is fire and a woman fuel.
Emiliano Zapata played by Marlon Brando in <u>Viva Zapata!</u> *(1952)*

PAST

Lloyd: There's only one catch to this business of going back to things.
Annie: What's that?
Lloyd: They never seem the same when you get back there.
Lloyd Richland/Rich Williams played by James Craig and Annie Goss played by Marjorie Main in <u>Gentle Annie</u> *(1944)*

Some things are best left in the past.
Jim Hammer played by Hal Holbrook in <u>The Legend of the Golden Gun</u> *(1979)*

A man can't escape his past.
Judge Benson played by Edgar Stehli in <u>No Name on the Bullet</u> *(1959)*

I'm trying to put some bad times behind me, but sometimes they don't stay put.
Charley Waite played by Kevin Costner in <u>Open Range</u> *(2003)*

Don't ask questions of the past. It has no answers for you.
Mrs. "Ma" Callum played by Judith Anderson in <u>Pursued</u> *(1947)*

PAST & FUTURE

What do you see out there, yesterday or tomorrow?
Jesse James/Tom Howard played by Willard Parker in <u>The Great Jesse James Raid</u> *(1953)*

I told you not to look backward. Look ahead.
Mrs. "Ma" Callum played by Judith Anderson in <u>Pursued</u> *(1947)*

Ma: You got the future to live for.
Jeb: I got the past to live with, too!
Mrs. "Ma" Callum played by Judith Anderson and Jeb Rand played by Robert Mitchum in <u>Pursued</u> *(1947)*

PAST & PRESENT

Please stop bringing back what we started out to be. We're what we are now.
Lela Wilson played by Mary Sinclair in <u>Arrowhead</u> (1953)

Things have a way of catching up with you.
Sunset Carson played himself in <u>El Paso Kid</u> (1946)

It isn't what a man has done in the past that matters. It's what he does in the present.
Fay Hollister played by Frances Dee in <u>Four Faces West</u> (1948)

What you've been means nothing. It's what you've become that's important.
Roger "Duke" Chadwick played by Kent Taylor in <u>Frontier Gambler</u> (1956)

PATHS

The raven keeps one eye on the future, yet one eye on the past, so his journey is always straight.
Grandpa/Old Pete Chasing Horse played by August Schellenberg in <u>Dreamkeeper</u> (2003)

I always make it a point to follow the path of least resistance.
Judge Worthington played by Ferris Taylor in <u>Mountain Rhythm</u> (1939)

PATIENCE

Patience, son, patience. The race is not to the swift, nor the battle to the strong.
Preacher Sims played by John Carradine, paraphrasing Ecclesiastes, in <u>Cain's Cutthroats</u> (1969)

There it goes! I have lost it. I have completely lost my patience! Has anyone seen my patience?
Ezechiel Gore played by Joe Stevens in <u>The Journeyman</u> (2001)

Do you remember your first lesson? It had to do with patience, the patience to wait until the time is right.
Jim Hammer played by Hal Holbrook in <u>The Legend of the Golden Gun</u> (1979)

PATRIOTISM

We all have to bear in mind that the practical side of patriotism is business.

Fat Gervin played by Walter Olkewicz in The Good Old Boys (1995)

PAWNS

When in doubt, sacrifice a pawn.

Sir John Applegate played by Roland Young in The Squaw Man (1931)

PEACE

There can be no peace if there is no good will to try it.

Tom Jeffords played by James Stewart in Broken Arrow (1950)

A man who preaches peace must practice it.

Senator Blakely played by Ward Bond in Dakota Incident (1956)

Peace doesn't come cheaply.

General Grant played by Hayden Rorke in Drum Beat (1954)

If I got peace at gunpoint, it wouldn't last.

Johnny MacKay played by Alan Ladd in Drum Beat (1954)

You can't get peace just wishing for it.

Johnny MacKay played by Alan Ladd in Drum Beat (1954)

The peace table often requires the sometimes unpleasant need to rely on the good faith of sometimes faithless enemies.

General Canby played by Warner Anderson in Drum Beat (1954)

To find peace one must believe in peace.

Many Horses played by Sheldon Peters Wolfchild in Miracle in the Wilderness (1991)

It takes two to make peace.

Sheriff Buck Hastings played by Willis Bouchey in No Name on the Bullet (1959)

All the riches in the world, señor, is not worth my peace of mind.
Don Esteban Valle played by Martin Garralaga in Song of the Gringo *(1936)*

We will not talk of right or wrong. We will talk of peace.
Taza played by Rock Hudson in Taza, Son of Cochise *(1954)*

Men always find reasons to avoid living in peace.
Dr. Henry Crowell played by Raymond Greenleaf in The Violent Men *(1955)*

The question beats in my head. Can a good thing come from a bad act? Can peace come from so much killing? Can kindness finally come from so much violence?
Pablo played by Lou Gilbert in Viva Zapata! *(1952)*

Peace is very difficult.
Emiliano Zapata played by Marlon Brando in Viva Zapata! *(1952)*

It seems like peace makes strange bedfellows.
Red played by Alex Sharp in Young Guns of Texas *(1962)*

PEONS

Everlasting patience is the life of a poor peon.
Don Ricardo played by Fred Coby in Don Ricardo Returns *(1946)*

PEOPLE

It's strange, isn't it, how one person can become so important in your life that, without them, nothing seems to matter.
Celia Wallace played by Catherine Craig in Albuquerque *(1948)*

George: I wish I was 10,000 miles from this place.
Marita: It wouldn't make any difference. You'd be the same wherever you were.
George Camrose played by Brian Donlevy and Marita Lestrade played by Rose Hobart in Canyon Passage *(1946)*

The only thing that tires me is people.
Woodfoot played by Lloyd Nolan in <u>The Last Hunt</u> (1956)

Santiago: People are worth more than money, more than land.
Maria: You are blind!
Santiago played by Arthur Kennedy and Maria played by Betta St. John in <u>The Naked Dawn</u> (1955)

People see what they want to see, and they say what they want to hear.
The Con Man played by Edward G. Robinson in <u>The Outrage</u> (1964)

There's nothing wrong with the land, just some of the people.
Kate Hollis played by Patricia Gaul in <u>Silverado</u> (1985)

Some people just don't have sense enough to get out of the rain.
Pop Apling played by Jim Davis in <u>Trail of Danger</u> (1977)

People aren't always as bad as you think.
Travis played by Terence Hill in <u>The Troublemakers</u> (1994)

PERCEPTION

I always say it ain't so much what you can do as what folks think you can do.
Windy Watkins played by Irving Bacon in <u>Drift Fence</u> (1936)

What people think is true is a lot more important than what really is true.
Noah Forbes played by Michael Callan in <u>The Magnificent Seven Ride!</u> (1972)

PERFECTION

Is it possible? Is it possible to improve on perfection?
The Kid played by Leonardo DiCaprio in <u>The Quick and the Dead</u> (1995)

PERSEVERANCE

We thought about it for a long time, endeavor to persevere. And when we had thought about it long enough, we declared war on the Union.
Lone Watie played by Chief Dan George in The Outlaw Josey Wales (1976)

There's an old saying, honey: 'Stick to your peanut stand even if you never sell a nut.'
Harry Weston played by Rory Calhoun in River of No Return (1954)

PERSONALITY

Smitty is a fart in a windstorm.
Otis played by Fred Dalton Thompson in Keep the Change (1992)

PERSPECTIVE

Will: You certainly have a strange point of view, Amos.
Amos: Yeah, well, when you ain't the lead dog, that's the point of view you get.
Will Cooper played by Lance Henriksen and Amos Russell played by M.C. Gainey in The Last Cowboy (2003)

When I was a child, I spoke as a child. I understood as a child. I thought as a child. But when I became a man, I put away childish things. For now we see through a glass, darkly.
McSween played by John Dierkes, paraphrasing the Bible, in The Left Handed Gun (1958)

We ain't so bad off. All we ain't got is money.
Chuckawalla played by Walter Brennan in The Texans (1938)

Maybe we're not half as bad off as we think we are.
Don Quixote Martindale played by Earle Hodgins in The Topeka Terror (1945)

One man's eye for beauty is another man's eyesore.
Roy Whitman played by John McIntire in Westward the Women (1952)

PESSIMIST

A pessimist is an optimist who is experienced.

Francis Leroy played by Francis Huster in <u>Another Man, Another Chance</u> (1977)

PHOTOGRAPHS

I don't reckon I can out-talk a photograph.

Brett Starr/Bill Brady played by Roy Rogers in <u>Bad Man of Deadwood</u> (1941)

PICKUP TRUCKS

The poor people of this state are dope fiends for pickup trucks. As soon as they get ten cents ahead, they trade in on a new pickup truck. The family's homestead, schools, hospitals, and happiness of Montana have been sold down the river to buy pickup trucks. There is a sickness here worse than alcohol and dope. It is the pickup truck debt. And there is no cure in sight.

Colson played by Joseph Spinell in <u>Rancho Deluxe</u> (1975)

PIPES

Through the pipe, man can send his voice to the invisible. The pipe is the link between man and earth and Wakan Tanka.

Wanagi played by Ron Soble in <u>The Mystic Warrior</u> (1984)

Pass him the peace pipe. Maybe that will shut him up!

The Medicine Man played by Cliff Solomon in <u>Shanghai Noon</u> (2000)

PLAIN FOLKS

They're just plain folks. I never shoot plain folks unless they really annoy me.

Lightning Jack Kane played by Paul Hogan in <u>Lightning Jack</u> (1994)

PLANS

Jim Bob: Now here's the plan. We go in the bank. And you go up to the teller and tell her you're robbing the bank. And then you rob the bank.
Cherokee Kid: You've been thinking about this plan for awhile, huh?
Jim Bob played by Walton Goggins and Isaiah/Cherokee Kid played by Sinbad in The Cherokee Kid (1996)

The best laid schemes of mice and men often go astray.
Lt. Richard Tufts played by Richard Webb, paraphrasing poet Robert Burns, in Distant Drums (1951)

Duchess: What the hell do we do now?
Charlie: Don't worry, I'll think of something. I always have. I've been in plenty of tight spots. I always get out of them on my own—my own brain, my own guts, the good sense that God gave me. I got into them on my own, and I'll get out of them on my own. Got any ideas?
Duchess/Amanda Quaid played by Goldie Hawn and Charlie Malloy played by George Segal in The Duchess and the Dirtwater Fox (1976)

Any plan makes room for trouble.
Dutchman played by Peter Graves in The Five Man Army (1969)

It's best to have a plan before you act.
Hawkeye played by Harry Carey in The Last of the Mohicans (1932)

You got to put your oar in and make for shore somewhere. Otherwise, you just drift.
Orion Clemens played by Greg Spottiswood in Roughing It (2002)

We really didn't expect the first part of the plan to work so we have no further plan. Sometimes you can over-plan these things.
Dusty Bottoms played by Chevy Chase in Three Amigos! (1986)

PLEASURE & SIN

I've heard it both ways. Pleasure is a sin and sin can be a pleasure.

The Preacher played by Chill Wills in <u>Gun Glory</u> (1957)

POEM

What is youth save promise?

What is age except regret?

The flowers we reap in May are from the seeds of April.

Trust is love unsaid.

Etta Place played by Elizabeth Montgomery in <u>Mrs. Sundance</u> (1974)

POKER

Poker ain't what you hold in your hand. It's how you play the hand that you hold.

The Gambler was uncredited in <u>The Animals</u> (1970)

PONDERING

I've been pondering on things so hard, I ain't had a chance to think.

Wilbur Clegg played by Gordon Jones in <u>Shoot-Out at Medicine Bend</u> (1957)

POPULARITY

I'm just about as welcome around these parts as smallpox right now.

Johnny Nelson played by James Ellison in <u>Call of the Prairie</u> (1936)

You never know how many people like you until you're dead.

Curly played by Gordon MacRae in <u>Oklahoma!</u> (1955)

POSITIVE THINKING

Things will seem better when there is daylight in the swamp.

Lynne Tilton played by Vera Ralston in <u>Timberjack</u> (1955)

POSSESSIONS

If you have nothing, then you don't have to worry about losing what you got.

Zack Stone played by Richard Joseph Paul in <u>Oblivion</u> (1994)

Possession is nine-tenths of the law.
Steve Haverly/The Durango Kid played by Charles Starrett in <u>Terror Trail</u> (1946)

You better hold on to the bird in your hand.
Chad Stevens played by Allan Lane in <u>The Topeka Terror</u> (1945)

If we want anything here, we got to fight hard to get it and twice as hard to keep it.
Dirk Breslin played by Rod McKuen in <u>Wild Heritage</u> (1958)

POSSIBILITY

Just because no one has done it doesn't mean it can't be done.
Tom Dunson played by James Arness in <u>Red River</u> (1988)

POTENTIAL

It is a small step. The seed is small. Maybe the tree will grow big.
Tom Jeffords played by James Stewart in <u>Broken Arrow</u> (1950)

POTHOLES

I've never seen a pothole one man can't dig.
Ry Weston played by Jon Voight in <u>Convict Cowboy</u> (1995)

POVERTY

America is supposed to welcome the poor, not gun 'em down!
Allen Stone played by David Lereaney in <u>Johnson County War</u> (2001)

We're so broke we can't pay attention!
Bill Doolin played by Bo Hopkins in <u>The Last Ride of the Dalton Gang</u> (1979)

POWER

In a violent country, he who seizes today controls tomorrow.
David Saxon played by Horst Frank in <u>The Grand Duel</u> (1972)

PRAYING

It always helped me find my way even when I was in doubt. It gives you answers to things you're confused about. It helps you find courage when you're afraid.
Seth Keller played by Daniel Quinn in <u>Miracle at Sage Creek</u> *(2005)*

Lord, make these sinners repent. If you can't make them repent, make them slow on the draw. If you can't make them slow on the draw, then make their powder wet. Thank you.
Beauregard Shelby/Preacher played by Rory Calhoun in <u>Mulefeathers</u> *(1977)*

Them who pray the loudest are the biggest hypocrites.
Dallas played by Terry Moore in <u>Rawhide</u> *(1959)*

PREACHERS

If I cannot rouse heaven, I intend to raise hell!
Reverend Joshua Sloan played by David Warner in <u>The Ballad of Cable Hogue</u> *(1970)*

We got a preacher that can sure make you smell brimstone!
Blue Duck played by Chill Wills in <u>Belle Starr</u> *(1941)*

I put my faith in the Good Book.
The Preacher played by Harry Belafonte (responding after pulling a gun out of a Bible and shooting the bad guy) in <u>Buck and the Preacher</u> *(1972)*

Ann: Tell me, how does a man go from the Jesuits to [gunfighter]?
Rafe: I couldn't get the knack of turning the other cheek.
Ann Rodney played by Virginia Madsen and Rafael "Rafe" Covington played by Tom Selleck in <u>Crossfire Trail</u> *(2001)*

He woke me up. They usually put me to sleep.
The Con Man played by Edward G. Robinson in <u>The Outrage</u> *(1964)*

I guess there's a little preacher in all of us as we get older.
Cap MacKellar played by Walter Brennan in The Showdown (1950)

Sometimes a preacher can bring a heap more comfort than a doctor.
Doc Parks played by Howard Wright in Stranger at My Door (1956)

Preacher: That diploma is just a piece of paper. I got my spiritual calling direct.
Jesse: That may be so, Sam. But all I got is your word on it.
Preacher Sam Shelby played by Chill Wills and Jesse Glendenning played by Robert Lowery in Young Guns of Texas (1962)

PREDICAMENT
There's a fly in the ointment.
Sheriff Tomas "Swede" Lundstrom played by Patrick Duffy in Desolation Canyon (2006)

PREDICTIONS
Never say what is about to be.
Charlie played by Gordon Tootoosis in Call of the Wild (1992)

Don't count your chickens before they're hatched.
Dave Wyatt/Steve Carson played by Dave O'Brien in Flaming Bullets (1945)

You can't tell how far a frog will jump by the way he squats.
Lucky Gosden played by Horace Murphy in Paroled—To Die (1938)

You never can tell from where you stand which way a frog will jump.
Hurricane Hattie McGuire played by Maude Eburne in West of the Badlands (1940)

PREJUDICE
It's always heartwarming to see a prejudice defeated by a deeper prejudice.
Mikey played by Stephen Lang in Lone Star (1996)

PREPARATION

You can't prepare if you fool yourself into thinking everything is all right.
Colonel Morsby played by Hugh Marlowe in <u>The Stand at Apache River</u> (1953)

PRESCRIPTIONS

No prescription ever helps any man unless he follows it.
Dr. Lee played by Frank Jaquet in <u>Call of the Rockies</u> (1944)

PRESSURE

Working under pressure is like a good strong wind at your back. It sort of pushes you along.
Eddie Dean played himself in <u>Prairie Outlaws</u> (1948)

PREVENTION

What I can see I can't prevent.
Sgt. Stuart played by Gregg Barton in <u>Gene Autry and the Mounties</u> (1951)

It's no good to lock the barn door after the horse is stolen.
Sam McCloud played by Dennis Weaver in <u>The Return of Sam McCloud</u> (1989)

A bit of prevention is always worth more than a lot of cure.
The Sheriff played by Horace Murphy in <u>The Stranger from Arizona</u> (1938)

PRICE

Is any price too great to pay for freedom and justice?
Margaret Lea played by Gail Patrick in <u>Man of Conquest</u> (1939)

Everything has a price.
Stevens played by Robert Frazer in <u>Pals of the Pecos</u> (1941)

PRIDE

Some people can afford pride and some can't.
Case Silverthorn played by Jim Davis in <u>The Gambler Wore a Gun</u> (1961)

When you've lost your pride, you've lost everything.
Madeline Hammond played by Jo Ann Sayers in <u>The Light of Western Stars</u> (1940)

There are times when one has to swallow one's pride to taste the finer fruits in life.
Maude Richards played by Sandy Gore in <u>Wrangler</u> (1989)

PRIMITIVE

Some men are more primitive than others, I guess. Some men just fight it harder.
Lucy Overmire played by Susan Hayward in <u>Canyon Passage</u> (1946)

PRINCIPLES

I believe history has taught us that men are only moral in terms of their own values.
Stephen Austin played by Patrick Duffy in <u>James A. Michener's Texas</u> (1995)

PRISON

I'm a lot safer inside than a lot of those that are on the outside.
Bill "Pinto Kid" Maywood played by Bill Cody in <u>Frontier Days</u> (1934)

PRISONER'S RIGHTS

The constitution says you can have a cigar. It don't say nothing about a light.
Deputy Ben was uncredited in <u>The Relentless Four</u> (1965)

PRIVATE AFFAIRS

My private affairs are private.
Frank Slayton played by Philip Carey in <u>Gun Fury</u> (1953)

A long time ago I made me a rule, ma'am. I never tell anybody what to do.
Hondo Lane played by Ralph Taeger in <u>Hondo and the Apaches</u> (1967)

PRIZES

The world is a rich prize, but you've got to go out and grab your share. It just doesn't come to you sitting at home.
Clay Clayburn played by James Craig in <u>Drums in the Deep South</u> (1951)

PROBLEMS

I love to hear about other people's problems. It makes me feel normal.
Phil Berquist played by Daniel Stern in <u>City Slickers II: The Legend of Curly's Gold</u> *(1994)*

There is no problem that cannot be solved at a conference table. All that is necessary is to sit down, man-to-man, face-to-face, and talk these problems out.
Senator Blakely played by Ward Bond in <u>Dakota Incident</u> *(1956)*

I'm always sure of my friend's problems, but not of my own.
Old Bailey played by Mickey Rooney in <u>Donovan's Kid</u> *(1979)*

I didn't say you had anything to do with it. I want to know what you're going to do about it.
Hopalong Cassidy played by William Boyd in <u>Forty Thieves</u> *(1944)*

There's always two ways to fix every problem.
Rafael Lopez played by J. Carrol Naish in <u>Thunder Trail</u> *(1937)*

PROGRESS

Businessman: You can't stop progress.
Kirby: That's right, but you can delay it.
The Businessman was uncredited and Kirby Morrow played by Bruce Cabot in <u>Rock Island Trail</u> *(1950)*

We would make better headway if we was walking backwards.
Ike played by Cliff Edwards in <u>Sagebrush Law</u> *(1943)*

Don't ever try to stop progress, son. Go with it. Be a part of it.
Gene Autry played himself in <u>Saginaw Trail</u> *(1953)*

PROMISES

People promise all sorts of things to the dying. It's been my observation they generally forget the whole business in a few days.
The Undertaker played by Ed Geldart in <u>Lonesome Dove</u> (1989)

What a man swears and what he does isn't always the same.
Chris Adams played by Yul Brynner in <u>Return of the Seven</u> (1966)

You can't spend promises.
Dan Thomas played by William Holden in <u>Texas</u> (1941)

They're heading for the Promised Land. I wonder how long they'll be able to live on promises.
Josh Tanner played by Robert Wagner in <u>White Feather</u> (1955)

PROMONTORY POINT

When they drive the golden spike we'll belong to both sides, and to each other.
Dave Brandon played by George O'Brien in <u>The Iron Horse</u> (1924)

PROMOTIONS

Make a man a corporal and he'll act like a sergeant, at least for the first few days.
Ben Zeigler played by Jim Davis in <u>Apache Warrior</u> (1957)

I'll make any trooper who gets killed corporal!
Bart Laish/Major Andrew Pepperis played by Sterling Hayden in <u>Arrow in the Dust</u> (1954)

Higher rank only means greater responsibility.
Captain Case McCloud played by George Montgomery in <u>Indian Uprising</u> (1952)

PROPHETS

A prophet is without honor in his own country.
Ahab Jones played by Peter Whitney in <u>The Great Sioux Uprising</u> (1953)

PROPOSALS

Clint: I'm asking you a question and the answer can't be maybe. It's got to be yes or no straight out. Understand? Will you marry me?

Felice: Oui, monsieur!

Clint Belmet played by Gary Cooper and Felice played by Lily Damita in Fighting Caravans (1931)

Belle: Will I have anything to say about this marriage?

Dana: Not until I ask you.

Belle Breckenridge played by Dorothy Malone and Dana Stribling played by Rock Hudson in The Last Sunset (1961)

California: I'd have married her if it hadn't been for one thing.

Jimmy: Yeah, what was that?

California: She said no.

California Carlson played by Andy Clyde and Jimmy Rogers played himself in Lumberjack (1944)

Don't let a pretty girl ask you twice, or an ugly one once.

Dick Summers played by Robert Mitchum in The Way West (1967)

PROs & CONs

Humphrey: Well, frankly, there are two schools of thought: pro and con.

President: Of course! But just how do they feel about it, pro and con?

Humphrey: Well, the pro people seem to be for it, and the con group are definitely against it.

Humphrey/Arthur Tyler played by Bob Hope and President Teddy Roosevelt played by John Alexander in Fancy Pants (1950)

PROSTITUTION & UNDERTAKERS

Is it a bigger sin to make a profit from dead bodies or living ones?

Undertaker Slidell played by Glenn Dixon in The Dalton Girls (1957)

PROTECTION

The weak always look for protection, not to get strong.
Steve Fallon played by Richard Basehart in <u>The Savage Guns</u> (1961)

PROXY

When you're me, don't get killed because I'm not ready to die yet.
Ramirez played by Nelson Eddy in <u>The Girl of the Golden West</u> (1938)

Braden: If you were drafted, why aren't you in the Army?
Farraday: Well, I am in a way. I hired a substitute for $300. Brave fellow, they tell me. I may even turn out to be a real war hero ... by proxy, of course.
Lt. Braden played by Craig Hill and James Farraday played by Van Johnson in <u>Siege at Red River</u> (1954)

PUBLIC OFFICE

But honesty and courage are not enough. Today, more than ever before, a public office calls for knowledge.
William Cantrell played by Walter Pidgeon in <u>Dark Command</u> (1940)

PUBLICITY

An Indian comes into my [detective] office and asks Rosetti to find a white man. I couldn't buy that kind of publicity!
Cesar Rosetti played by Barney Phillips in <u>Savage Run</u> (1970)

PUNISHMENT

'And where the offence is let the great axe fall.'
Jack Pickett played by Gary Busey, quoting Shakespeare, in <u>Ghost Rock</u> (2003)

If you jail him, you got to feed him. Horse whipping is cheaper.
Claude Henderson played by Anthony Jochim in <u>Joe Dakota</u> (1957)

The more punishment you take, the tougher you get.
Banner Cole played by Audie Murphy in <u>Posse from Hell</u> (1961)

PURCHASES

Don't buy an old wagon just because it's new painted.
Flapjack Kate played by Marjorie Main in <u>Big Jack</u> *(1949)*

PURGATORY

Refuge is where the marginally good are gleaned from the hopelessly wicked.
Brooks/Jesse James played by John David Souther in <u>Purgatory</u> *(1999)*

PURPOSE

A man just drifts when he's without illusion, without purpose in life.
Logan Cates played by Rory Calhoun in <u>Apache Territory</u> *(1958)*

You have found something worth living for. I envy you.
Catherine played by Catherine Spaak in <u>Take a Hard Ride</u> *(1975)*

PUSHING

Why do you want to push things until they break?
Marshal Cotton Ryan played by Robert Ryan in <u>Lawman</u> *(1971)*

I can be pushed just so far and no further!
Egbert Floud played by Charles Ruggles in <u>Ruggles of Red Gap</u> *(1935)*

QUALITIES

I want to be proud of you, of what you do. But I can't be if you think that to be a big man you have to throw away all the qualities I loved in your life.
Janet Calvert played by Terry Moore in <u>Cast a Long Shadow</u> *(1959)*

Kirby has such a wealth of manners and such a poverty of ethics.
David Strong played by Grant Withers in <u>Rock Island Trail</u> *(1950)*

You're the most beautiful girl in the whole world. You got everything! Of course, some of the things you got you'd be better off without, but you got everything.
Waldo played by Andy Devine in <u>The Traveling Saleswoman</u> *(1950)*

QUALITY & QUANTITY

It ain't how many that you're up against you got to worry about, you know. It's who they are.
John Henry Lee played by Willie Nelson in <u>Once Upon a Texas Train</u> *(1988)*

QUEST

The ultimate quest has no ending. That is what gives the quest its ultimate value.
Kwai-Chang Caine played by David Carradine in <u>The Gambler Returns: The Luck of the Draw</u> *(1991)*

QUESTIONS & ANSWERS

You ever notice how a fella keeps repeating the question when he's stalling about answering?
Laredo Stevens played by Bruce Cabot in Angel and the Badman (1947)

The best way to get an answer is to ask a question.
Dan Barton/Jack Bruce played by George Montgomery in Last of the Badmen (1957)

You're liable to find out some things that you wouldn't want to know.
The Henchman was uncredited in Rainbow Valley (1935)

When you ask questions, you got to wait for answers.
Sheriff Chris Hamish played by William Conrad in The Ride Back (1957)

QUICK DRAW

There's nothing wrong with a man trying to outdraw himself in the mirror.
Lee Hackett played by Van Heflin in Gunman's Walk (1958)

He seemed to be faster'n death itself.
Prologue in The Longest Hunt (1968)

QUITTING

Coke: Do you always quit when you're ahead?
Jim: Well, I can't think of any better time.
Coke Beck played by David Carradine and Jim Killian played by Glenn Ford in Heaven with a Gun (1969)

RABBIT'S FOOT

I'm legally leaving you everything I own. There's my lucky rabbit's foot.
California Carson played by Andy Clyde, making last wish before hanging, in Riders of the Deadline (1944)

RACE

Black men carrying guns. That's a white folks' nightmare.
Jonathan Henry played by Paul Winfield in The Blue and the Gray *(1982)*

You see, the [black] boy was poorly raised. His folks filled his head with all kinds of fool thoughts that he was just as good as the normal man.
Mr. Doyle played by Frank McRae in Lightning Jack *(1994)*

It seems to me the only problem that a white man has with a colored man is that he's afraid. A lot of people are always afraid of what they don't understand.
"Little J" Teeters played by Stephen Baldwin in Posse *(1993)*

We'll stop at the next telephone and send someone after you. This bus is for Indians only.
Santana played by Eddie Little Sky in Savage Run *(1970)*

What skin has been chosen for Paradise? What is the color of an immortal soul?
Father Junipero Serra played by Michael Rennie in Seven Cities of Gold *(1955)*

These people, they smile at me and show their teeth. But it's the eyes that bite.
Elena de la Madriaga played by Linda Cristal in Two Rode Together *(1961)*

RAILROADS

Wes: I always did want an engineer's watch.
Reno: What for? They're never on time!
Wes McQueen played by Joel McCrea and Reno Blake played by John Archer in Colorado Territory *(1949)*

You've built too many railroads. Your thinking is getting warped. You're beginning to believe that everything has to move in a straight line.
Del Stewart played by William Bishop in Overland Pacific *(1954)*

Big trains don't wait for small passengers.
Sir John Applegate played by Roland Young in <u>The Squaw Man</u> (1931)

RAINBOWS

I have my own rainbows to chase.
Clancy played by Jack Thompson in <u>The Man from Snowy River</u> (1982)

RANCH

A ranch. You know, a lot of ground with a sky over it.
Stephanie Lock played by Fay McKenzie in <u>Cowboy Serenade</u> (1942)

You can't run a ranch on good intentions.
Gregg Jackson played by Onslow Stevens in <u>Sunset Serenade</u> (1942)

RANK

It is tribal law that rank has its privileges.
Chief Sitting Bull played by John War Eagle in <u>Tonka</u> (1958)

REACH

Peg: He's beyond reach.
Hollis: No one ever is.
Peg Jarret played by Patricia Medina and Hollis Jarret played by Macdonald Carey in <u>Stranger at My Door</u> (1956)

READINESS

Keep your powder dry.
Orrin Sackett played by Tom Selleck in <u>The Sacketts</u> (1979)

READING

Don't believe everything you read.
Hopalong Cassidy played by William Boyd in <u>Border Vigilantes</u> (1941)

People believe what they read.
Frank James played by Bill Paxton in <u>Frank & Jesse</u> (1994)

Once you can read, you can have every adventure you ever dreamed of. In the pages of a book, you are a princess in a tower or the best shot in the West. In those pages, there are no limits to where you can go, who you can be with. And no one will ever tell you that you're too young to slay the dragon because it happens right here where it's safe.
Marty Claridge played by Katherine Heigl in <u>Love Comes Softly</u> (2003)

REALITY

You can't think about what might be. You have to deal with what is.
Clara Allen played by Barbara Hershey in <u>Return to Lonesome Dove</u> (1993)

It's not the way things look—it's how they are.
Hannah Lund played by Liv Ullmann in <u>Zandy's Bride</u> (1974)

REASON

A reasonable man always settles for a half, a quarter, or whatever he can get.
Dan Kehoe played by Clark Gable in <u>The King and Four Queens</u> (1956)

REBORN

It's got to be that a person can be born new if they want to.
Gentry/John Coventry played by Fred MacMurray in <u>Quantez</u> (1957)

Sometimes it is better to drink the soup of forgetfulness to cross the river to be reborn on the other side.
Li Ping played by Kim Chan in <u>Thousand Pieces of Gold</u> (1991)

RECIPIENT

It's always worse to be the recipient.
Blackie Jobero played by Cesar Romero in <u>The Beautiful Blond from Bashful Bend</u> (1949)

RECKONING

What shall you do on the day of reckoning?
Luke played by Jason Rodriguez in Reckoning (2002)

RECONSTRUCTION

As the old saying goes, anybody can break an egg but nobody can put the pieces back together.
Honest Plush Brannon played by Wallace Beery in Barbary Coast Gent (1944)

There's nothing ever destroyed that can't be rebuilt.
Benjamin Trane played by Gary Cooper in Vera Cruz (1954)

REFERENCE

When a man doesn't want to give reference, he usually has something to hide.
Jeff played by Robert J. Wilke in Smoky (1966)

REFORM

Molly: What's reform mean?
Hopalong: Oh, I guess it's just sort of doing things that other people think you should do.
Molly Rand played by Charlene Wyatt and Hopalong Cassidy played by William Boyd in Borderland (1937)

REGRET

Philio: You won't regret it, I promisc.
Bret: My pappy always told me to stay clear of men who promise no regrets.
Philio Sandeen played by Stuart Margolin and Bret Maverick played by James Garner in Bret Maverick: The Lazy Ace (1981)

Regret is a terrible thing to take to the grave.
Tom Partridge played by Max Gail in Sodbusters (1994)

REGULATIONS

Regulations say that I can't hit you, but they do allow me to remove obstacles that get in my way!
Captain Webb Calhoun played by Rod Cameron in <u>Oh! Susanna</u> (1951)

REGULATORS

They ain't nothing but a rich man's hired law.
Dooley played by William Forsythe in <u>Dollar for the Dead</u> (1998)

REHABILITATION

I guess hanging him will straighten him out.
Sheriff Romero played by George Baxter in <u>Gun Battle in Monterey</u> (1957)

You can't make a lily-white dove out of a desert hawk.
Nosey played by Sidney Toler in <u>Heritage of the Desert</u> (1939)

Brady: I mean to go straight. Just like an axe gets dull, you can sharpen it again.
Sheriff: If it's good steel.
Brady Sutton played by Philip Carey and Sheriff McVey played by Roy Roberts in <u>Wyoming Renegades</u> (1955)

REINTEGRATION

I guess you can't break out of prison and into society in the same week.
Ringo Kid played by John Wayne in <u>Stagecoach</u> (1939)

RELATIONSHIPS

He'd rather be cheated on by me than married to you.
Brandy played by Mari Blanchard in <u>Destry</u> (1954)

Duchess: What do you got in mind?

Charlie: Nothing! I swear to God! Not a thing! I just want to lie here and enjoy the quiet, the river, the view, the sky, trees, the leaves—maybe fool around a little.

Duchess/Amanda Quaid played by Goldie Hawn and Charlie Malloy played by George Segal in The Duchess and the Dirtwater Fox (1976)

Miner: You know, the Chinese say you should have only one true love in your entire life; otherwise, you are no better than a mangy dog or a loose woman.

Joe: Good thing I'm not Chinese.

The Chinese Miner played by Warwick Yuen and Joe Byrne played by Orlando Bloom in Ned Kelly (2003)

RELATIVES

It's bad luck to shoot your own relatives.

Jim Hedge played by Clem Bevans in Loaded Pistols (1948)

You can pick your friends but not your relatives.

Hopalong Cassidy played by William Boyd in Unexpected Guest (1947)

REMEMBERING

I always remember what is worth remembering.

Peso played by Gilbert Roland in Apache War Smoke (1952)

REPENT

It's surprising how easy it is to get a man to repent when he thinks he's going to shake hands with the Lord.

Dr. Jonathan Mark played by Walter Brennan in Singing Guns (1950)

REPUTATION

A woman's reputation is all she has. There's no forgiveness for women. A man may lose his honor and begin it again, but a woman cannot.

Dona Alfonsa played by Miriam Colon in All the Pretty Horses (2000)

There's some things that even soapy water can't wash away.
Billy Joe Cudlip played by Lee Van Cleef in <u>*Beyond the Law*</u> *(1967)*

A boy looking for a reputation is the most dangerous thing alive.
Mister played by Ben Johnson in <u>*Bite the Bullet*</u> *(1975)*

Lucy: Mark, my reputation!
Mark: Well, the secret will die with me on the battlefield.
Lucy: Promise?
Lucy was uncredited and Mark Geyser played by Michael Horton in <u>*The Blue and the Gray*</u> *(1982)*

My reputation is all I got and it ain't for sale!
Calamity Jane played by Anjelica Huston in <u>*Buffalo Girls*</u> *(1995)*

His reputation convicted him.
Josiah Lowe played by Dean Jagger in <u>*The Hanged Man*</u> *(1974)*

There ain't no place far enough for you to outride your reputation.
Ben Thompson played by Stillman Segar in <u>*The Last of the Fast Guns*</u> *(1958)*

My only mistake was in thinking I could run away from a reputation.
Frame Johnson played by Ronald Reagan in <u>*Law and Order*</u> *(1953)*

A man's reputation travels far these days, especially if it's bad.
Duke Dillon played by Jack LaRue in <u>*The Law Rides Again*</u> *(1943)*

Many a time the reputation is a lot bigger than the man.
Wild Bill Hickok played by William "Wild Bill" Elliott in <u>*North from the Lone Star*</u> *(1941)*

I have the best collateral in the world: my reputation!
Chris Mooney played by Barry Sullivan in <u>*Texas Lady*</u> *(1955)*

RESERVATIONS

Why don't they stay on the reservation where they belong?
Gene Autry played himself in <u>The Cowboy and the Indians</u> *(1949)*

RESISTANCE

Shouldn't a man resist the hand that's chocking him to death?
Stephen Austin played by Otto Kruger in <u>The Last Command</u> *(1955)*

A man only has so many no's in him.
Helen Carter played by Myrna Dell in <u>Roughshod</u> *(1949)*

RESOURCEFULNESS

A man's got to use the tools he can lay his hands on.
Fred Winslow played by Henry Hull in <u>Colorado Territory</u> *(1949)*

RESPECT

A man who respects another asks him to do something. A man who disrespects another tells him to do something.
Keenan Deerfield played by Lou Diamond Phillips in <u>The Trail to Hope Rose</u> *(2004)*

RESPONSIBILITY

Every man has got to pull his weight.
Mose played by Abraham Benrubi in <u>Open Range</u> *(2003)*

It's a great responsibility to ask men to fight, perhaps to die.
Don Hernan played by Fernando Rey in <u>The Savage Guns</u> *(1961)*

RESULTS

Losses don't count! What counts is results! The troops are paid to defend their county.
The Colonel was uncredited in <u>A Pistol for Ringo</u> *(1965)*

RETREAT

Now I'm not one to show the white feather, but even the best military leader knows when to fall back and count his losses.
Cap played by Denver Pyle in Gunpoint (1966)

RETRIBUTION

He's dead! What more do you want from him?
Getz played by Dan Duryea in The Hills Run Red (1966)

REVENGE

Revenge always turns sour.
Hildy played by Stella Stevens in The Ballad of Cable Hogue (1970)

Revenge is a cold trail made.
Sheriff Tomas "Swede" Lundstrom played by Patrick Duffy in Desolation Canyon (2006)

What's the good of revenge even against the most vile crime? A few moments of bitter satisfaction, perhaps one instance of certainty.
Donald McRae played by Yves Renier in The Other Side of the Law (1995)

Son, I'm asking you again to give up this idea of revenge. You're not only hurting others but you're hurting yourself as well. You're not a man anymore. You're just a ball of hate that's eating you up, just like a rotten spot eats up an apple.
Cap MacKellar played by Walter Brennan in The Showdown (1950)

REVOLUTIONS

Revolutions are for money. That's what starts them and that's what comes out of them.
Tom Bryan played by Rory Calhoun in The Treasure of Pancho Villa (1955)

REWARD

Well, I ain't splitting [the reward] more than five ways. In fact, I was hoping that kid would get lucky and shoot a couple of us.
Jake played by Don Collier in El Diablo (1990)

RIDING

Lacey: Well, can you ride or not?

Jimmy: Hell, yeah, I can ride. I was riding when I fell off.

Lacey Rawlins played by Henry Thomas and Jimmy Blevins played by Lucas Black in All the Pretty Horses *(2000)*

There never was a horse that couldn't be rode, never a cowboy that couldn't be throwed.

J.W. Coop played by Cliff Robertson in J.W. Coop *(1971)*

RIFLE

This old rifle of mine ain't too choosy about who she shoots.

Sam Kendrick played by Stacy Keach in Desolation Canyon *(2006)*

RIGHT

Remember famous quotation: 'Any man more right than all his neighbors make majority of one.'

Secret Agent Fong played by Mako, quoting Henry David Thoreau, in The Great Bank Robbery *(1969)*

Doing right is better than looking right.

Mrs. Clell Miller played by Anne Barton in The Great Northfield, Minnesota Raid *(1972)*

You're so full of what's right, you can't see what's good.

H.C. Curry played by Cameron Prud'Homme in The Rainmaker *(1956)*

RIGHT & WRONG

He usually manages to do the wrong thing at the right time.

Cheyenne Davis played by Lash La Rue in Border Feud *(1947)*

No one is ever all wrong, and no one is ever all right.

Brady Hawkes played by Kenny Rogers in Gambler V: Playing for Keeps *(1994)*

Things ought to be simple. They ought to be right or wrong, not someplace in between.
Steve Burden played by Guy Madison in The Hard Man *(1957)*

Being wrong don't hold danger for a man who ain't never been right in his whole life.
Frank Jesse played by Dan Duryea in Six Black Horses *(1962)*

I don't see how anyone can look so right and think so wrong.
Colt Saunders played by Charlton Heston in Three Violent People *(1956)*

RIGHTEOUSNESS

The righteous are too smug and satisfied with themselves to doubt their own judgment.
George Ives played by Clayton Moore in Montana Territory *(1952)*

RISK & REWARD

In the words of the immortal poet, a man who will not take a chance winds up without a seat in his pants.
Honest Plush Brannon played by Wallace Beery in Barbary Coast Gent *(1944)*

Colonel: Do you expect me to believe that you would risk a firing squad just to see a girl?
Captain: Well, you met her. What do you think?
Colonel Jeb Britten played by Bruce Bennett and Captain Vance Britten played by Ronald Reagan in The Last Outpost *(1951)*

If the risk is little, the reward is little.
Jack Beauregard played by Henry Fonda in My Name Is Nobody *(1973)*

The guys that take all the risks take all the profits.
Larry Kimball played by Smith Ballew in Panamint's Bad Man *(1938)*

ROADS

Norfolk: And how was the shorter road?

Luke: Longer.

Norfolk played by Ian Bannen and Luke Matthews played by James Coburn in <u>Bite the Bullet</u> (1975)

Caine: Many roads often lead to the same place.

Sheriff: Many roads lead to places where no one wishes to go.

Kwai Chang Caine played by David Carradine and Sheriff Mills played by Luke Askew in <u>Kung Fu: The Movie</u> (1986)

This stretch of road runs between nowhere and not much else.

Wesley Birdsong played by Gordon Tootoosis in <u>Lone Star</u> (1996)

A man's got to go down the road he thinks is the road he's got to go down.

O.B. Taggart played by Mickey Rooney in <u>Outlaws: The Legend of O.B. Taggart</u> (1994)

The grass is always greener down the road.

Texas Grant played by Tim McCoy in <u>Texas Cyclone</u> (1932)

The road of the outlaw closes all others.

Caption in <u>The Toll Gate</u> (1920)

But I do know that for the most part, my life has been filled with crossroads. And recently, I've made some few bad turns.

Matt Cooper played by Kenny Rogers in <u>Wild Horses</u> (1985)

ROBBERY

How many want to live? Hold up your hands, please!

The Bandido Leader played by Joby Baker in <u>The Adventures of Bullwhip Griffin</u> (1967)

We had a lot less than we needed, and he had a lot more than he needed.

Hard Case played by Pepper Martin in <u>Cahill: United States Marshal</u> (1973)

It's better to give than receive, ain't it folks?
Tommy played by Harrison Ford in The Frisco Kid (1979)

A fair exchange is no robbery.
Sunset Carson played himself in Santa Fe Saddlemates (1945)

ROCK BOTTOM
That's about as low as a man can get until they bury him.
Cass Dowdy played by Leo Gordon in The Night of the Grizzly (1966)

ROGERS, WILL
I never met a man I didn't like.
Inscription on statue of Will Rogers in The Story of Will Rogers (1952)

ROLES
She was so busy being a lady that she forgot to be a woman.
John Henry Thomas played by John Wayne in The Undefeated (1969)

ROMANCE
My daddy told me that romance was one part bourbon and two parts fantasy.
Zack Hollister played by Brian Bloom in Brotherhood of the Gun (1991)

Your head is so full of romance, you don't even have no room for the truth in there.
Janet Conforto played by Janice Rule in Kid Blue (1973)

ROOTS
My whole life I've never had roots deeper than topsoil.
Rafael "Rafe" Covington played by Tom Selleck in Crossfire Trail (2001)

For a logger, you sure don't know much about roots.
Sheriff Taylor played by Regis Toomey in Guns of the Timberland (1960)

Anything that ties you down is no good.
Duke Hudkins played by John Wayne in <u>A Lady Takes a Chance</u> (1943)

Grass can't grow without roots.
Gene Autry played himself in <u>Springtime in the Rockies</u> (1937)

ROPES

When you find yourself on one end of a rope in this country, you want to be sure there's a friend on the other.
Kitty Baldwin played by Dorothy Wilson in <u>When a Man's a Man</u> (1935)

ROUGHNESS

Don't treat 'em too rough; just barely kill them.
Mike McComb played by Errol Flynn in <u>Silver River</u> (1948)

RULES

You ride with us, you ride by our rules!
Digger played by Morgan Sheppard in <u>Gunsmoke: Return to Dodge</u> (1987)

Before you start making up your own rules, learn to respect the rules of others.
Principal played by Dennis St. John in <u>Warrior Spirit</u> (1994)

RUNNING AWAY

You can't run away from yourself.
Fay Hollister played by Frances Dee in <u>Four Faces West</u> (1948)

If you're running out on somebody, you're running out on yourself.
Tom Dooley played by Michael Landon in <u>The Legend of Tom Dooley</u> (1959)

A body doesn't have to get on a horse and ride a thousand miles to run away. She can run away right down a flight of cellar steps.
Wes Steele played by Ray Milland in <u>A Man Alone</u> (1955)

SACRIFICE

Isn't it strange how everything worthwhile in life is made possible only by sacrifice?
Fay Hollister played by Frances Dee in <u>Four Faces West</u> (1948)

SAFETY

There's a difference between playing it safe and being an old woman.
Norman played by Jack Elam in <u>Firecreek</u> (1968)

Sometimes a dangerous jump leads a man to safety.
Eddie Dean played himself in <u>Stars Over Texas</u> (1946)

'From this nettle, danger, we pluck this flower, safety.'
Dr. Joseph McCord played by John McIntire, quoting Shakespeare, in <u>The Tin Star</u> (1957)

SALESMANSHIP

Waldo: In one town I got two orders.
Mabel: Well, that's better than nothing. What were they?
Waldo: Get out and stay out!
Waldo played by Andy Devine and Mabel King played by Joan Davis in <u>The Traveling Saleswoman</u> (1950)

SALOONS

Jean: If they let it stay open, someone is bound to get shot.
Brit: What will happen if they close it?
Jean: They're afraid it might kill the whole town.
Jean McLane played by Ann Summers and Brit Marshall played by Tim Holt in The Avenging Rider (1943)

I'm usually thrown out of much nicer places than that.
Chito Rafferty played by Richard Martin in Border Treasure (1950)

Ethan: Hey, is there any good place to eat around here?
Bartender: Well, yeah, right here! The food's no good but the beer is cold!
Ethan played by Rick Rossovich and George the Bartender was uncredited in The Gambler Returns: The Luck of the Draw (1991)

There'll be no brawls here, gentlemen, unless they're over me.
Cherry Malotte played by Anne Baxter in The Spoilers (1955)

Waldo: We better get out of here before we get shot!
Mabel: We'll have to hurry. I'm half shot already!
Waldo played by Andy Devine and Mabel King played by Joan Davis in The Traveling Saleswoman (1950)

SALVATION

I just ain't ready to be saved yet.
Hildy played by Stella Stevens in The Ballad of Cable Hogue (1970)

Don't save one son at the expense of another.
Sarah Frye played by Sandra Nelson in Brothers of the Frontier (1996)

You can't force salvation on people.
Captain Frank Minardi played by Terry O'Quinn in Heaven's Gate (1980)

SAVAGES

Sometimes it's hard to tell who the savages are.
Lester White played by Dewey Martin in *Savage Sam* *(1963)*

SEA

He said it was so big the mind couldn't hold it.
Elias Hooker played by Ralph Waite in *Chato's Land* *(1972)*

SEARCHING

I still say you are searching for fruit in a barren orchard.
Padre José played by Eduard Franz in *The Last of the Fast Guns* *(1958)*

SECRETS

Your secret was as quiet as the thunder.
Cochise played by Jeff Chandler in *Broken Arrow* *(1950)*

In my country we have a saying: A secret whispered in a coffee house is as confidential as a headline in a newspaper.
Elya Carlson played by Anita Ekberg in *4 for Texas* *(1963)*

Mary: I think he secretly likes you.
Haven: He's a man who can certainly keep a secret.
Mary Caslon played by Agnes Moorehead and Haven played by Dick Powell in *Station West* *(1948)*

SECURITY

Come a rainy day, a man sometimes needs more than just a slicker.
Sheriff Abel Rose played by Morgan Woodward in *Gunsmoke: To the Last Man* *(1992)*

SELF-FULFILLING PROPHECY

Ned: See, I told you I couldn't do it!

Crecencio: Yes, you told me you couldn't do it. But first, you told yourself. You said, 'I can't do it.' And so you could not.

Young Ned Blessing played by Sean Baca and Crecencio played by Luis Avalos in <u>Lone Justice</u> *(1994)*

SELF-PRESERVATION

Self-preservation is the first law of nature.

Sam Enders played by Tom Chatterton in <u>Lawless Empire</u> *(1945)*

SELF-RELIANCE

If a fellow don't look after himself, nobody else will.

Sam Slade played by Bob Burns in <u>Belle of the Yukon</u> *(1944)*

If you want something done, you do it yourself.

Henry Logan played by John P. Ryan in <u>Blood River</u> *(1991)*

SELF-RESPECT

It feels good to get up off my knees.

Sheriff O'Hea played by Edgar Buchanan in <u>Coroner Creek</u> *(1948)*

If you don't think anything of yourself, how do you expect anybody else to?

Pat Brennan played by Randolph Scott in <u>The Tall T</u> *(1957)*

Alex: You're looking for a meal, huh?

Will: No, I'm looking for a job.

Alex played by Ben Johnson and Will Penny played by Charlton Heston in <u>Will Penny</u> *(1968)*

SELF-WORTH

Marty: The Bible says there's good in every one of us.

Secora: The Bible was written before I was born.

Marty Robbins played himself and Secora played by Joyce Redd in Ballad of a Gunfighter (1964)

SENTIMENT

The price of sentiment comes high.

Colonel George Armstrong Custer played by Philip Carey in The Great Sioux Massacre (1965)

SEPARATION

There's nothing like a little separation to make the heart grow fonder.

Cora Redding played by Miranda Otto in The Jack Bull (1999)

SEX

Considering the sex of parrots, I've had little practical experience, Mr. Hatfield. But I'm told there's one infallible test. It's like this: place a small piece of fried bacon on the ground in front of the parrot whose sex is in doubt. If he picks it up, it's a male. And if she picks it up, it's a female.

Butterworth played by John Beck in Billy the Kid (1930)

Carmel: Randy, we must remember, I'm a missus.

Randy: And I, my dear, am a mister.

Carmel played by Tina Louise and Mayor Randolph Wilker played by Martin Balsam in The Good Guys and the Bad Guys (1969)

Most men have a habit of forgetting the other side of the deal once they get what they want.

Kaitlin Mullane played by Crystal Bernard in Siringo (1994)

SHADOWS

Don't you ever try to run away from your shadow. It can't be done.
The Stranger played by Jim Davis in <u>*The Badge of Marshal Brennan*</u> *(1957)*

You cast a mighty long shadow of your own.
Chip Donohue played by John Dehner in <u>*Cast a Long Shadow*</u> *(1959)*

My brother's shadow has walked away.
Taza played by Rock Hudson in <u>*Taza, Son of Cochise*</u> *(1954)*

Gene: Meet me tonight at Signal Rock. And be sure nobody follows you.
Smiley: I won't even bring my shadow along with me.
Gene Autry played himself and Smiley Burnette played himself in <u>*Winning of the West*</u> *(1953)*

SHEEP

Sheep who are lost cannot be expected to find the shepherd.
Sarah Jones played by Jean Parker in <u>*The Parson and the Outlaw*</u> *(1957)*

SHOOTING

Gutierrez: You know, you did not have to shoot him six times.
Sheriff: Five times. If it bothers you, I'll pray for him.
Gutierrez played by Al Lettieri and Sheriff Sean Kilpatrick played by Richard Harris in <u>*The Deadly Trackers*</u> *(1973)*

That cowpoke can shoot faster than his own shadow.
Virgil played by Neil Summers in <u>*Lucky Luke*</u> *(1991)*

Duke: Why don't you look where you're shooting?
Willoughby: I don't know. I guess I'm not inquisitive.
Duke played by Bud Abbott and Willoughby played by Lou Costello in <u>*Ride 'Em Cowboy*</u> *(1942)*

Not every situation calls for your patented approach of shoot first, shoot later, shoot some more, and then when everybody's dead try to ask a question or two!
Artemus Gordon/President Ulysses S. Grant played by Kevin Kline in <u>Wild Wild West</u> *(1999)*

Nurse: You wouldn't shoot.
Shuck: Lady, I castrate sheep with my teeth for a living. There's no telling what I'm capable of.
The Nurse played by Marquetta Senters and Shuck played by Kris Kristofferson in <u>Wooly Boys</u> *(2003)*

SICKNESS

It's occurred to me that the real sicknesses, the most important ones, are seldom physical.
John Gant played by Audie Murphy in <u>No Name on the Bullet</u> *(1959)*

I have never been sick, fatally sick, a day of my life.
Dr. Rufus Tate/Bates played by Earle Hodgins in <u>Santa Fe Marshal</u> *(1940)*

SIDEKICKS

Bill and me was so close we just wore one hat for the two of us!
Gabby Hayes played by George "Gabby" Hayes in <u>Calling Wild Bill Elliott</u> *(1943)*

I'd still trade the two of 'em for one good cigar!
Wade Hatton played by Errol Flynn in <u>Dodge City</u> *(1939)*

I told him he was nothing without me. Maybe I'm nothing without him.
Clay Blaisdell played by Henry Fonda in <u>Warlock</u> *(1959)*

SIDELINES

Sometimes you can see more from the sidelines than the man bulldogging the steer.
Zeb Smith played by William "Wild Bill" Elliott in <u>Hellfire</u> *(1949)*

SIDES

For the first time in my life, I'm all mixed up. I got a friend on one side, and a good friend on the other side.
Jim Sherwood played by Brian Donlevy in <u>Billy the Kid</u> (1941)

You can't just sit on the front porch and fan yourself. You're going to have to pick a side.
Frank Norton played by William Phipps in <u>Gunfight in Abilene</u> (1967)

There's always two sides to a story.
Hopalong Cassidy played by William Boyd in <u>In Old Colorado</u> (1941)

I don't take sides with trash against trash.
Mitch Barrett played by Alan Ladd in <u>One Foot in Hell</u> (1960)

If you're not with us that means you're against us.
Martin White played by Leo Gordon in <u>Seven Angry Men</u> (1955)

SIGNS

The Finest Comes No More If You Have To Buy The Cheapest Twice
Wagon sign in <u>Adios Amigo</u> (1975)

Need for a sign is for the weak of faith.
Growling Bear played by Gordon Tootoosis in <u>Into the West</u> (2005)

Doctor McGuinness—Teeth Pulled While You Wait
Town sign in <u>The Lady from Cheyenne</u> (1941)

Hopen For Business
Saloon sign in <u>Nevada</u> (1997)

SILENCE

Sometimes silence is the best answer you can give a person.
Mary Ann Young played by Mary Astor in <u>Brigham Young</u> (1940)

If there's anything I can't stand it's a lot of noisy silence.
Charlie Anderson played by James Stewart in <u>Shenandoah</u> (1965)

SIMPLICITY

Lucy: Don't complicate things. Let's keep them simple and straight.
George: My thoughts rarely travel in a straight line.
Lucy Overmire played by Susan Hayward and George Camrose played by Brian Donlevy in <u>Canyon Passage</u> (1946)

A simple pleasure. It's the secret to life: finding joy in the simple things.
Quentin Leech played by Kenny Rogers in <u>Rio Diablo</u> (1993)

SIN

Preacher: You, boy! Have you been a sinning?
Youth: No, sir! I try but I guess I'm just not old enough.
The Preacher played by Bob Gunton and Young Ned Blessing played by Sean Baca in <u>Lone Justice</u> (1994)

There's no wilderness wide enough to hide a sin.
Father Simon played by Morgan Farley in <u>The Wild North</u> (1952)

SINCERITY

Linc: Just to show you my heart is in the right place.
Mike: Well, it'll take an autopsy to prove that to me.
Lincoln "Linc" Corey played by Jim Davis and Mike Prescott played by Forrest Tucker in <u>California Passage</u> (1950)

SINGING

Oh, I don't reckon your voice will stampede the herd.
Matt Doniphon played by William Farnum in <u>Public Cowboy No. 1</u> *(1937)*

It's the first time I ever seen a fellow chloroform himself with his own singing.
Judge Gabby Whittaker played by George "Gabby" Hayes in <u>Sheriff of Tombstone</u> *(1941)*

It's hard to sing and be mean at the same time.
Gene Autry played himself in <u>Springtime in the Rockies</u> *(1937)*

SIZE

He walks too tall for his size.
Curly Ringo played by John Archer in <u>Best of the Badmen</u> *(1951)*

A lot of little things add up to big things.
Duchess played by Marin Sais in <u>The Fighting Redhead</u> *(1949)*

He's so darn big, he's surrounded mostly by himself.
Innskeep played by Charley Grapewin in <u>Gunfighters</u> *(1947)*

SLAVERY

[Slavery] is the systematic coercion of one group of men over another.
Lt. Colonel Joshua Lawrence Chamberluin played by Jeff Daniels in <u>Gods and Generals</u> *(2003)*

Do you think the only slaves are in the South?
Dr. Noah Banteen played by Carl Benton Reid in <u>Stage to Tucson</u> *(1950)*

Slavery is an economic issue, not a moral one.
Georgia Lawshe played by Angelina Jolie in <u>True Women</u> *(1997)*

SLICK

You're slicker than snot on a doorknob!

Cary played by Frederic Forrest in <u>*The Missouri Breaks*</u> *(1976)*

SMART

When you're trying to outsmart a man, don't pick one that's smarter than yourself.

Duke Dillon played by Dennis Moore in <u>*Colorado Serenade*</u> *(1946)*

I'm getting too smart for one man. I ought to incorporate.

Professor Hatch played by Lee "Lasses" White in <u>*Dude Cowboy*</u> *(1941)*

At least I'm smart enough to know myself.

Dan Hammond played by Robert Ryan in <u>*Horizons West*</u> *(1952)*

SMILE

She can smile without making it a simper. That's a rare quality in a woman.

Frank Slayton played by Philip Carey in <u>*Gun Fury*</u> *(1953)*

SOCIETY

I couldn't miss this gala opening. Why, the cream of society is here, and a little of the skimmed milk too.

Effie Tinker played by Ellen Lowe in <u>*Rancho Grande*</u> *(1940)*

SOLDIERS

An officer's efficiency is weakened by every man who likes him personally. The instant personality enters a military organization, discipline goes out the window.

Major Frank Archer played by George Montgomery in <u>*Battle of Rogue River*</u> *(1954)*

Mostly, a soldier fights for his outfit. He's proud of it and doesn't want to let it down.

Miles Archer played by Guy Madison in <u>*The Charge at Feather River*</u> *(1953)*

Without the sound of the guns to ride to, I'm lost.
Lt. Colonel George Armstrong Custer played by Wayne Maunder in <u>Crazy Horse and Custer: The Untold Story</u> (1967)

Every soldier in a war doesn't have to believe in what he's fighting for. Most of them fight just to back up the other soldiers in their squad. They try not to get them killed. They try not to get them extra duty. They try not to embarrass themselves in front of them.
Colonel Delmore Payne played by Joe Morton in <u>Lone Star</u> (1996)

If there's one thing worse than an officer, it's someone who sucks up to an officer.
Marauder was uncredited in <u>A Reason to Live, A Reason to Die</u> (1972)

I'm an officer and gentleman by Act of Congress, an officer and gentleman. So you keep your mouth shut!
Lt. William Fowler played by Tab Hunter in <u>They Came to Cordura</u> (1959)

If you want a man to be a good soldier, you must treat him like one.
Captain Mark Bradford played by Cornel Wilde in <u>Two Flags West</u> (1950)

There are times when the individual soldier is much more effective than the unit.
Major Howell Brady played by Jeff Chandler in <u>War Arrow</u> (1954)

SOLIDARITY

One twig might bend but the bundle will always remain strong.
Grandpa/Old Pete Chasing Horse played by August Schellenberg in <u>Dreamkeeper</u> (2003)

There is no word in our language for me or I ... just we, us.
Grandpa/Old Pete Chasing Horse played by August Schellenberg in <u>Dreamkeeper</u> (2003)

SOLITUDE

There's nothing wrong with quiet.
Jeremiah Johnson played by Robert Redford in <u>Jeremiah Johnson</u> (1972)

SONS & FATHERS

Why is it when a guy hates his old man as much as I do, you still keep trying to do that one thing that he'll be proud of?
Bernard played by David Roya in Billy Jack (1971)

I always used to think there was too much of me in you for us to hit it off. But I know now that that was wrong. There wasn't enough of me in you!
Matthew Devereaux played by Spencer Tracy in Broken Lance (1954)

He did not hate you because you were a gunfighter. He hated you because you were not there.
Pearl played by Sandrine Holt in Gunslinger's Revenge (2005)

A man must walk out of his father's shadow to find the light.
Aleta Burris played by Viveca Lindfors in The Halliday Brand (1957)

The apple doesn't fall too far from the tree.
Overstreet played by Jack Palance in Keep the Change (1992)

It's never too late for a son to come to his dad with his troubles.
Timothy "Pop" Owens played by Edward Van Sloan in Riders of the Rio Grande (1943)

A son is a man's immortality.
Lt. Gresham played by James Douglas in A Thunder of Drums (1961)

SOPHISTICATION

Sophistication is of the mind, not the heart.
John Delmont played by John Dehner in When the Redskins Rode (1951)

SORE LOSER

If anything happens to me, kill him!
Colonel Tom Rossiter played by Richard Widmark in Alvarez Kelly (1966)

SORRY

Davis: I'm sorry.

Matt: Sorry gets it once.

Davis Healy played by Bruce Boxleitner and Matt Dillon played by James Arness in
Gunsmoke: One Man's Justice (1994)

SOULS

You're just freezing my soul. That's what you're doing, freezing my soul.

John McCabe played by Warren Beatty in McCabe & Mrs. Miller (1971)

Souls don't always enjoy perfect health, you know, anymore than bodies do.

Josiah Dozier Gray played by Joel McCrea in Stars in My Crown (1950)

SPACE

It ain't that we don't like people. We like room more.

Big Eli Wakefield played by Burt Lancaster in The Kentuckian (1955)

SPAGHETTI WESTERNS

In the sixties, they started making these spaghetti westerns. I was always jealous
of these guys because they had better background music than we did. And they
all got to wear those great raincoats, even when it was 110 [degrees] in the
shade. But the trouble was, you could hardly understand anything they said.

Narration by Peter/Town Drunk played by G.W. Bailey in Rustlers' Rhapsody (1985)

SPEECHES

Well, I seem to remember my father telling me on an occasion somewhat
similar to this: 'Be brief, be sincere, and be seated.'

Mike McComb played by Errol Flynn in Silver River (1948)

SPIRITS

Sergeant: They think the chief turned into a bird.

General: Shoot the bird down, Sergeant.

The Sergeant was uncredited and General George Armstrong Custer played by Robert Shaw in Custer of the West (1968)

The American West was settled in a spirit of courage, determination, and friendship. The Old West may be gone, but the spirit survives.

Prologue in 8 Seconds (1994)

Like the trees in the wind, you'll be able to feel me. I'll always be there.

Jim Hammer played by Hal Holbrook in The Legend of the Golden Gun (1979)

Though we cannot see those that are dear to us, it does not mean they are no longer with us. Keep your parents alive within you and their spirits will never die.

The Indian Chief was uncredited in The Legend of the Lone Ranger (1981)

The spirit ain't worth spit without a little exercise.

The Preacher played by Clint Eastwood in Pale Rider (1985)

A man without spirit is whipped.

Coy LaHood played by Richard Dysart in Pale Rider (1985)

Let not your spirit quail because your stomach is empty.

Professor Pandow played by Earle Hodgins in The Singing Cowboy (1936)

SPIT

He wouldn't spit on you if you were on fire!

Caitlin Jones played by Marcy Walker in The Return of Desperado (1988)

SPOILS OF WAR

To the victor belong the spoils.

Joseph Lee played by Ossie Davis in The Scalphunters (1968)

SPRINGTIME

I guess spring is the time that makes you think of faraway and long ago.
Annie Oakley played by Barbara Stanwyck in Annie Oakley (1935)

STAGECOACHES

Why the hell do they call it the noon stage? Half the time it don't get in before sundown!
James Pepper played by Ben Johnson in Chisum (1970)

It's so exciting sitting up there holding those reins right in your two hands. Why, you can almost see your thoughts traveling right down your lines to your leaders.
Lucky Jenkins played by Russell Hayden in Stagecoach War (1940)

STAGNATION

People who stay put have no place to go.
Van Morgan played by Dean Martin in 5 Card Stud (1968)

STAMPEDES

The bigger the herd, the easier the stampede.
Candy Johnson played by Clark Gable in Honky Tonk (1941)

STANDS

There's some things a man has to do if he's going to live with himself.
Gil Reardon played by Robert Knapp in Gunmen from Laredo (1959)

A man has got to stand sometime.
Vincent Bronson played by Lee J. Cobb in Lawman (1971)

There's a time in every man's life when he must face himself.
Rev. Jericho Jones played by Charles "Buddy" Rogers in The Parson and the Outlaw (1957)

STAR

My father always said: 'Little one, hitch your wagon to a star.'
Julia Lawrence played by Teresa Wright in <u>California Conquest</u> (1952)

STATE OF MIND

Being out in the world is a state of mind, not of geography.
Rupert Venneker played by Peter Ustinov in <u>The Sundowners</u> (1960)

STATUES

They don't put up a statue for live men.
Lem Shaver played by Al Bridge in <u>The Last Musketeer</u> (1952)

STEALING

I stole that money fair and square!
Jack Cooper played by Craig Sheffer in <u>The Desperate Trail</u> (1995)

They'd steal the pennies off a dead man's eyes.
Langdon Towne played by Robert Young in <u>Northwest Passage</u> (1940)

STOMACH

An empty stomach will make a man do a lot of things he wouldn't do otherwise.
Eddie Dean played himself in <u>Prairie Outlaws</u> (1948)

The impediment of the heart is the stomach.
Emiliano Zapata played by Marlon Brando in <u>Viva Zapata!</u> (1952)

The way to a man's heart is through his stomach.
Desprit Dan played by George "Gabby" Hayes in <u>War of the Wildcats</u> (1943)

STORMS

It's always calm before a storm.
Judge Roy Bean played by Robert McKenzie in <u>Sing, Cowboy, Sing</u> (1937)

STRANGERS

It's funny how you can live so close to somebody all your life and never really get to know them.
Tim Taylor played by Tim Holt in <u>Brothers in the Saddle</u> (1949)

Sometimes it's easier to talk to a stranger.
Santiago played by Arthur Kennedy in <u>The Naked Dawn</u> (1955)

It isn't where you are that makes you a stranger. It's where you think you're a stranger that makes you one.
Fred Tiflin played by Shepperd Strudwick in <u>The Red Pony</u> (1949)

STRATEGIES & TACTICS

They aim to shoot it out. Shorty, you and me will keep under cover. And Ofie, you surround the house!
Pappy played by Lloyd "Slim" Andrews in <u>Cowboy Serenade</u> (1942)

When you're surrounded and haven't a chance, attack!
John Devlin played by John Wayne in <u>Dakota</u> (1945)

We can get a lot more flies with honey than we can with vinegar.
Roy Rogers played himself in <u>The Far Frontier</u> (1949)

I say we just ride over there and shoot the whole damn bunch of 'em!
Leola Borgers played by Gregory Scott Cummins in <u>Lone Justice II</u> (1995)

Together we are few; separated we are many.
Prince Hannoc played by Jon Hall in <u>When the Redskins Rode</u> (1951)

STRENGTH

To know your fear is to acquire wisdom. And from wisdom will come strength.
Six Eyes was played by Apesanahkwat in <u>Gunsmoke: One Man's Justice</u> (1994)

Fear is eternal darkness. Go instead with inner strength. For it is like a deep river into which all streams flow. It increases, always moving forward, and soon there is nothing that can stand in its way.
Master Po played by Keye Luke in Kung Fu: The Movie (1986)

STUBBORNNESS

When are you going to stop trying to talk horse sense into mules?
Sheriff Abel Rose played by Morgan Woodward in Gunsmoke: To the Last Man (1992)

I discovered a long time ago you can't make a woman do something she doesn't want to do.
Cadmus Cherne played by Victor McLaglen in Many Rivers to Cross (1955)

I'm a stubborn man. I guess it's from working with pack mules so much. But the more people push me one way, the more I want to go the other.
Jess Collins played by Howard Duff in Sierra Stranger (1957)

STUPIDITY

Jack: Just how stupid do you think I am?
Wild Bill: I don't know. I just met you.
Jack McCall played by Garret Dillahunt and Wild Bill Hickok played by Keith Carradine in Deadwood (2004)

I imagine you're a pretty good judge of stupidity.
Jeffrey Carson played by George O'Brien in Hollywood Cowboy (1937)

I might be stupid but I ain't no idiot!
Judy Canova played herself in Oklahoma Annie (1952)

SUCCESS

Don't grow old waiting for success to catch up with you.
Rusty Joslin played by Raymond Hatton in Cowboys from Texas (1939)

You'll be traveling the road to success in no time. You're just on a little detour now.
Gene Autry played himself in <u>Home in Wyomin'</u> (1942)

SUFFERING

Just because you suffered in your life doesn't give you the right to take it out on the people around you.
The Priest played by Ted Haler in <u>Uninvited</u> (1993)

SUICIDE

And if you do decide on suicide, be good enough not to do it on the premises. It's bad for business, you know.
Fenner played by Ron Whelan in <u>Kangaroo</u> (1952)

SUNDOWNER

A sundowner is someone whose home is where the sun goes down. It's the same as saying someone who doesn't have a home.
Sean Carmody played by Michael Anderson in <u>The Sundowners</u> (1960)

SUNSHINE

It's amazing what a little bit of sun will do to a man's disposition.
John Danaher played by Glenn Ford in <u>Border Shootout</u> (1990)

We Indians are taught that sunshine is the best medicine of all.
Alessandro played by Don Ameche in <u>Ramona</u> (1936)

SUPERSTITION

Who was it that said superstition is the religion of feeble minds?
Father Garcia played by Cesar Romero in <u>Lust in the Dust</u> (1985)

SUPPLY & DEMAND

Any stock is worthless unless someone is willing to pay for it.
Ben Calhoun played by Dale Robertson in <u>Scalplock</u> (1967)

SURVIVAL

Everything in the forest kills something else to stay alive itself. Animals kill other animals for food. A large tree will kill a smaller tree to have more room for its roots. There's death all over the forest. Men get used to living with it, women don't.
Captain Jedediah Horn played by George Montgomery in Fort Ti (1953)

I was never his woman. He did what he wanted. I did what I had to do.
Helen Ramirez played by Maria Conchita Alonso in High Noon (2000)

The future of my people is not fighting with the white man but living with him.
Wise Eagle played by Ralph Moody in Pawnee (1957)

Does a drowning man ask what kind of wood is in a plank that floats by?
Ed Halcomb played by Jess Barker in The Peacemaker (1956)

SWORDS

Don Diego: Do you know how to use that thing?
Alejandro: Yes! The pointy end goes into the other man.
Don Diego de la Vega/Zorro played by Anthony Hopkins and Alejandro Murrieta played by Antonio Banderas in The Mask of Zorro (1998)

Esteban: Is your blade as sharp as your tongue?
Don Diego: Is yours as dull as your wit?
Esteban played by Ron Leibman and Don Diego Vega/Zorro played by George Hamilton in Zorro, the Gay Blade (1981)

TALENT

Luck is always family with talent.
Sheriff Tomas "Swede" Lundstrom played by Patrick Duffy and Sam Kendrick played by Stacy Keach in Desolation Canyon (2006)

You got a rare talent but you're not letting yourself use it. You got a feel for life, boy. Don't fight it. Let it lead you.
Jim Hammer played by Hal Holbrook in The Legend of the Golden Gun (1979)

TALES

People make up a lot of things. Sometimes even I don't know what really happened. I know this though: stories are always better.
Wyatt Earp played by Kevin Costner in Wyatt Earp (1994)

TALKING

Finished or just out of breath?
Jimmy Ryan played by Guy Madison in The Beast of Hollow Mountain (1956)

Men who claim they just want to talk generally have more than just words on their mind.
Cy Whitaker played by Richard Hamilton in Bret Maverick: The Lazy Ace (1981)

Sometimes I think your tongue is hung on a hinge.
Ma Hardy played by Emma Dunn in <u>Cowboy from Brooklyn</u> (1938)

Pilar here is the perfect match for Ben. He don't talk much and she never stops.
Lana played by Beverly D'Angelo in <u>Lightning Jack</u> (1994)

It always makes me feel better to let things breathe a little, not bury 'em.
Sue Barlow played by Annette Bening in <u>Open Range</u> (2003)

If you can't say nothing, don't speak.
Sacha Bozic played by S.Z. Sakall in <u>San Antonio</u> (1945)

I've found that if you talk as much as I do, it's best to say very little.
J. Horatio Boggs played by Hobart Cavanaugh in <u>Stage to Chino</u> (1940)

Don Diego: This is my servant, Paco. He is a mute. He cannot speak.
Esteban: Oh, excellent! Perhaps he will give lessons to my wife.
Don Diego Vega/Bunny Wigglesworth played by George Hamilton and Esteban played by Ron Leibman in <u>Zorro, the Gay Blade</u> (1981)

TASKS

Liking it and doing it are two different things.
Billy Bucklin played by David Figlioli in <u>Hard Ground</u> (2003)

Before I start anything, I always say to myself: now if the worst thing happens, will it be worth it? And if I figure it is, I go right ahead.
Sam Mayhew/Tom Blackwell played by Skip Homeier in <u>The Road to Denver</u> (1955)

Don't start something you can't finish.
Slim Carter/Hughie Mack played by Jock Mahoney in <u>Slim Carter</u> (1957)

TEACHING

When you teach a man how to kill, how can you unteach him?
Jake was uncredited in <u>Payment in Blood</u> (1968)

TEARS

What was it Sir Walter Scott said, 'and love is the lovliest when embalmed in tears'?
Rose Griffith played by Angela Stevens in <u>Jack McCall, Desperado</u> (1953)

All men are suckers for tears, except me. I'm waterproof.
The Con Man played by Edward G. Robinson in <u>The Outrage</u> (1964)

TELEGRAMS

A telegram never seems to bring good news.
July Johnson played by Chris Cooper in <u>Return to Lonesome Dove</u> (1993)

TEMPER

Now you calm down. You'll get a more harmonious outcome.
Rafael "Rafe" Covington played by Tom Selleck in <u>Crossfire Trail</u> (2001)

Don't let no axe fly off no handle!
Sgt. Monday Wash played by Irving Bacon in <u>Fort Ti</u> (1953)

My mother always told me to count to ten before I lost my temper.
Brant played by Jim Bannon in <u>Frontier Revenge</u> (1948)

TEMPERANCE

A man is tempered by his setbacks, not by his victories.
Dr. Jonathan Mark played by Walter Brennan in <u>Singing Guns</u> (1950)

TEMPTATION

I never could resist temptation.
Clint Allison played by Cameron Mitchell in <u>The Tall Men</u> (1955)

TESTS

There comes a time in every man's life when he's just got to stick his hand in the fire and see what he's made of.
John McCabe played by Warren Beatty in <u>McCabe & Mrs. Miller</u> (1971)

TEXAS

There's plenty of room out there for every dream I've ever had.
Davy Crockett played by Fess Parker in <u>Davy Crockett, King of the Wild Frontier</u> (1955)

There's room enough down there for a man to stretch his soul as well as his legs.
Samuel "Sam" Houston played by Richard Dix in <u>Man of Conquest</u> (1939)

THIEVES

There's no honor among thieves.
Steve Haverly/The Durango Kid played by Charles Starrett in <u>Terror Trail</u> (1946)

THINKING

Remember what Shakespeare said: 'There's nothing good or bad, but thinking makes it so.'
Jeffrey Carson played by George O'Brien in <u>Hollywood Cowboy</u> (1937)

Gus: I better go with you. Somebody's got to do the thinking.
Jed: All right, you do the thinking but I'm doing the talking!
Gus played by James Whitmore and Jed Cooper played by Victor Mature in <u>The Last Frontier</u> (1955)

Sometimes it helps to think out loud.
John Carter played by Stan Ivar in <u>Little House: Bless All the Dear Children</u> (1983)

Maybe you will live longer if you don't think quite so loud.
Manuel played by Charles Stevens in <u>The Renegade Ranger</u> (1938)

I sometimes use my head for something else besides putting my hat on.
Smiley Burnette played himself in <u>Whirlwind</u> (1951)

THREATS

Don't threaten a man while you're down.
Johnny Reno played by Dana Andrews in <u>Johnny Reno</u> (1966)

Never threaten anybody with an empty gun.
Fulton played by Marshall Reed in <u>Rough, Tough West</u> (1952)

TIME

Any fool can get old, Hunter. It takes a genius not to waste time.
Marvin Fishinghawk played by Gordon Tootoosis in <u>The Doe Boy</u> (2001)

'To every thing there is a season, and a time to every purpose under the heaven.'
Kathy Summers played by Barbara Payton, quoting the Bible, in <u>Drums in the Deep South</u> (1951)

Time wounds all heals.
S. Quentin Quale played by Groucho Marx in <u>Go West</u> (1940)

There's always a time and a place for everything.
Mayor John Blaine played by Paul Everton in <u>Gun Law</u> (1938)

After awhile, time is the most important thing.
Tom Healy played by Anthony Quinn in <u>Heller in Pink Tights</u> (1960)

Time is a commodity running into short supply.
Corporal Kenneally played by Stuart Graham in <u>One Man's Hero</u> (1999)

To a fly who lives only one day, ten minutes can be a long time.
Winnetou played by Pierre Brice in <u>Rampage at Apache Wells</u> (1965)

Kid: Is a year so long a time?

Manuel: With my last wife, a day was a long time.

The Kid played by Keith Larsen and Manuel played by Frank Puglia in <u>*Son of Belle Starr*</u> *(1953)*

Time is a healer.

Lt. General Winfield Scott played by Sydney Greenstreet in <u>*They Died With Their Boots On*</u> *(1941)*

TIMES

Times change and I'm not much at changing with them.

Peg Guthrie played by Lea Thompson in <u>*Montana*</u> *(1990)*

TOASTING

To your feet, ma'am. They're almost as big as your mouth.

The Stranger played by Clint Eastwood in <u>*High Plains Drifter*</u> *(1973)*

To them that have their roads ahead.

Ace Bonner played by Robert Preston in <u>*Junior Bonner*</u> *(1972)*

To our two romantics. To one who sees what is, and to one who sees what can be. Lord, grant that the two are compatible.

Banjo Paterson played by David Bradshaw in <u>*The Man from Snowy River*</u> *(1982)*

TODAY

We have today, perhaps tomorrow, but never yesterday.

Jim Wingate/James Carston played by Warner Baxter in <u>*The Squaw Man*</u> *(1931)*

Yesterday's dead and gone; take care of today.

Nancy Warren played by Martha Hyer in <u>*Wyoming Renegades*</u> *(1955)*

TOMBSTONES

To live in the hearts of others is not to die.
Tombstone Inscription in Ghost Rock (2003)

Murdered by a traitor and a coward whose name is not worthy to appear here.
Tombstone inscription in The Last Days of Frank and Jesse James (1986)
Comment: The murderer gets more mention than Jesse does, and it's Jesse's tombstone!

TOWNS

Do you want a good town? Then you got to prune the sick branches.
Rev. Griffin played by Arthur Shields in Apache Drums (1951)

A town is only as good as the people in it.
Jack Wright played by Fred MacMurray in At Gunpoint (1955)

Town criers always know something.
Waldo Peek played by Robert Anderson in Buchanan Rides Alone (1958)

But if the town changed for the worse, it could change for the better. Now all it needs is a little faith, courage, and conviction.
Eli Bloodshy played by Jim Dale in Hot Lead and Cold Feet (1978)

It's a nice town. Small enough to be comfortable but large enough to have a future.
Dr. Luke Canfield played by Charles Drake in No Name on the Bullet (1959)

TRACKING

He could follow a trail underwater.
Scat Russell played by Pat Buttram in Gene Autry and the Mounties (1951)

Hawken could track a leaf back to its place on the tree.
Noel Hickman played by Chuck Pierce, Jr., in Hawken's Breed (1987)

You couldn't find teeth on a comb!
Marshal Windy Halliday played by George "Gabby" Hayes in <u>Renegade Trail</u> (1939)

I can track any animal. I can track spiders. I can track lizards and snakes. I can track fleas and bugs. But I cannot follow the tracks in books.
Famous Shoes played by Wes Studi in <u>Streets of Laredo</u> (1995)

TRADEOFF

For every way of living there's something that has to be given up.
Jim Bridger played by Van Heflin in <u>Tomahawk</u> (1951)

TRAGEDY

Tragedy, like human life itself, must have a beginning, a middle, and an end.
Narration in <u>The Great Sioux Massacre</u> (1965)

TRAILS

We all get off on the wrong trail once in awhile.
Breck Coleman played by John Wayne in <u>The Big Trail</u> (1930)

Sooner or later, a man rides a one-way trail he can't turn back on.
Steve Allen/The Durango Kid played by Charles Starrett in <u>The Blazing Trail</u> (1949)

Daddy used to say that you never knew a man until you rode the trail with him.
Zack Hollister played by Brian Bloom in <u>Brotherhood of the Gun</u> (1991)

Every time I open a new trail, I like to think that others will follow.
Hawkeye played by Randolph Scott in <u>The Last of the Mohicans</u> (1936)

The further you get up a trail, the harder it is to turn back.
Larry Kerrigan played by Johnny Mack Brown in <u>Montana Moon</u> (1930)

TRAITORS

It is not easy to recognize a traitor among your own.
Rubriz played by Joseph Calleia in Branded (1951)

TRAPS

It looks like he got caught in his own trap.
Red Barton played by Dick Foran in Blazing Sixes (1937)

You can't expect to catch a fox by showing him the trap first.
Bill Foster played by Drake Smith in Cattle Queen (1951)

Sometimes the cat closes its eyes to fool the mouse.
Captain Gonzales played by George J. Lewis in Twilight on the Rio Grande (1947)

TRAVEL

He travels fast who travels alone.
Bob Blake played by Herbert Jeffries in Harlem Rides the Range (1939)

Pee Wee: Napoleon said an army travels on its stomach.
Doc: As far as I was concerned, I'd rather travel on a horse.
Pee Wee McDougal played by Snub Pollard and Doc Thornton played by Horace Murphy in Riders of the Rockies (1937)

TREASURES

I'm not going home with bulging bags of gold. But I'm a lot richer than when I started. I found wealth in things like a warm fire when it's freezing; the beauty of snow-capped peaks; the companionship of a noble dog; the love of a wonderful woman; and the strength, the port, and the friendship of a wise Indian guide and counselor. These are the treasures I am taking from this land. And I feel like the richest man in the world.
Narration by John Thornton played by Rich Schroder in Call of the Wild (1992)

'Lay not up for yourselves treasures on earth, but lay up for yourselves treasures in heaven.'
Pilot Pete played by Art Smith, quoting the Bible, in The Painted Hills *(1951)*

TRESPASSING

Everybody steps on somebody else's toes sometimes.
Sheriff Buck Hastings played by Willis Bouchey in No Name on the Bullet *(1959)*

There are none who trespass against us as we trespass against ourselves.
Sam Christy played by Jeff Chandler in The Plunderers *(1960)*

TRIALS

Danny: We'll get a fair trial, won't we?
J.D.: Lots of men get a fair trial and hang.
Danny Cahill played by Gary Grimes and J.D. Cahill played by John Wayne in Cahill: United States Marshal *(1973)*

TROUBLE

Why don't you go out and eliminate your troubles instead of standing around talking about them?
Sunset Carson played himself in Alias Billy the Kid *(1946)*

I got troubles enough on my own without looking for more.
Jim Walker played by Rory Calhoun in Apache Uprising *(1966)*

Things don't settle, Abel. They get settled.
Matt Dillon played by James Arness in Gunsmoke: To the Last Man *(1992)*

Trouble brings people together.
Daniel Halliday played by Joseph Cotton in The Halliday Brand *(1957)*

Running from trouble won't get rid of it.
Tim Holt played himself in Hot Lead *(1951)*

It's a lot easier to start trouble than it is to stop it.
Billy Carson played by Buster Crabbe in <u>Oath of Vengeance</u> (1944)

I only know one way to face trouble: head on!
The Baltimore Kid played by Fred Astaire in <u>The Over-the-Hill Gang Rides Again</u> (1970)

I'm not here to make trouble. I'm here to end it.
Don Murdock played by Edward LeSaint in <u>The Stranger from Texas</u> (1939)

If you're looking for trouble, you're liable to find it.
Reno played by Edward Brady in <u>Thunder in the Desert</u> (1938)

Trouble seems to follow you around.
Gene Autry played himself in <u>Valley of Fire</u> (1951)

When trouble comes, they come not single spies but in battalions.
Chavez Y. Chavez played by Lou Diamond Phillips, paraphrasing Shakespeare, in <u>Young Guns II</u> (1990)

TRUST

You can't always trust a fellow by the way he looks.
Rocky Lane played by Allan Rocky Lane in <u>Bandit King of Texas</u> (1949)

Trust in the Lord and wait until you can make every shot count!
Rev. Rosenkranz played by Arthur Shields in <u>Drums Along the Mohawk</u> (1939)

It's wise to know a man before you place your trust in him.
The Lone Ranger played by Clayton Moore in <u>The Lone Ranger</u> (1956)

You put too much trust in words, Roy. Now we put our trust in action.
Tacona played by Keith Richards in <u>North of the Great Divide</u> (1950)

Nobody will ever trust a mailman who lost his first letter.
Russell played by Russell Hicks in <u>Plainsman and the Lady</u> (1946)

Make your peace signs with one hand and keep your rifles ready in the other.
Gene Autry played by himself in <u>Ride, Ranger, Ride</u> (1936)

Martin: So you left [him] alone in the house?
Janey: Yes, sir. There wasn't nothing worth stealing, so I figured I could trust him.
Martin played by Frank Wilcox and Janey Nolan played by Betty Brewer in <u>Wild Bill Hickok Rides</u> (1942)

TRUTH

The truth isn't always pleasant.
John Allen played by William Welsh in <u>Beyond the Rockies</u> (1932)

I never really lied to you, Etta. I just kind of held off telling the truth every now and then.
Sundance Kid played by Brett Cullen in <u>Gambler V: Playing for Keeps</u> (1994)

How many times must you listen to the truth before you believe it?
Padre José played by Eduard Franz in <u>The Last of the Fast Guns</u> (1958)

The truth never hurt an innocent man.
Ben Sadler played by Jeff Chandler in <u>Man in the Shadow</u> (1957)

When in doubt, tell the truth.
George Washington McLintock played by John Wayne in <u>McLintock!</u> (1963)

I think the time is never right for a man to tell his wife the truth.
Martha played by Jesse Colter in <u>Stagecoach</u> (1986)

U V

ULTIMATUM

If I don't leave here with it, I'm not going to leave here without it.
Matt Fletcher played by Marlon Brando in <u>The Appaloosa</u> *(1966)*

UNCERTAINTY

Sometimes when a person don't know what to do, the best thing is to just stand still.
Gay Langland played by Clark Gable in <u>The Misfits</u> *(1961)*

UNDERSTANDING

It is good to understand the ways of others.
Tom Jeffords played by James Stewart in <u>Broken Arrow</u> *(1950)*

It isn't given to us to understand some things, I reckon.
Adam Naab played by J. Farrell MacDonald in <u>Heritage of the Desert</u> *(1932)*

Hopkins: Is that lucid?
Wilson: Oh sure, but it isn't quite clear yet.
Banker Hopkins was uncredited and Chuck Wilson played by Hoot Gibson in <u>The Last Outlaw</u> *(1936)*

Sometimes it ain't so good to understand.
Smoky Joe Miller played by Charles "Chic" Sale in <u>Men of America</u> (1932)

Nella: You're gonna have to bend down a little with them words if you want me to understand.
Nathan: Why don't you try reaching up instead?
Nella Turner played by Jane Russell and Nathan Stark played by Robert Ryan in <u>The Tall Men</u> (1955)

UNIFORMS

It's fascinating, señora, what a uniform can conceal.
Colonel Stuart Valois played by John Mills in <u>Chuka</u> (1967)

You may have been a soldier once, but you're just a grocery clerk now.
Edward Janroe played by David Dukes in <u>Last Stand at Saber River</u> (1997)

USEFULNESS

I've always known a rolling stone was worth two in a bush.
California Carlson played by Andy Clyde in <u>Lost Canyon</u> (1942)

VALUE

Whitey: I'll guard it with my life.
Henry: Ah, can you do better than that, Whitey?
Whitey Haber played by Ed Begley, Jr., and Henry Moon played by Jack Nicholson in <u>Goin' South</u> (1978)

If something is easy to get, people don't care about it. They don't value it. But if it's hard to get, well, then you've got something.
Kay Weston played by Marilyn Monroe in <u>River of No Return</u> (1954)

A wise man once said that nothing was of value until it was tried and tested by fire.
Homer "Doc" Brown played by William Powell in <u>The Treasure of Lost Canyon</u> (1952)

A man saves what he values most.
Major Ives played by Warner Anderson in <u>*The Yellow Tomahawk*</u> *(1954)*

VENGEANCE

Vengeance is a bitter thing, my child. It can destroy the avenger as well.
Father Antonio played by Martin Garralaga in <u>*Bandit Queen*</u> *(1950)*

Vengeance is a hollow pursuit.
Zack Stone played by Richard Joseph Paul in <u>*Oblivion*</u> *(1994)*

VENOM

One of these days, you're going to die of your own venom.
Belle played by Vera Ralston in <u>*Belle Le Grande*</u> *(1951)*

VERANDA

Belle: You can have anything you want out on the veranda.
Gus: Well, that's a pretty broad statement that takes in a lot of territory, Belle.
Belle Aragon played by Annelle Hayes and Guthrie "Gus" McCabe played by James Stewart in <u>*Two Rode Together*</u> *(1961)*

VICES

You are a strange man, Rio. You have no vices: no wine, no women, not even talk. If a man should kill you, he should not aim at your heart.
José Esqueda played by Anthony Quinn in <u>*Ride, Vaquero!*</u> *(1953)*

VICTIMS

He didn't seem to care if I knifed him or not. He's all right!
William Parcell Candy played by Jonathan Haze in <u>*Five Guns West*</u> *(1955)*

Sieber: You are getting screwed!
Horn: It happens to everybody sooner or later if you live long enough.
Al Sieber played by Richard Widmark and Tom Horn played by David Carradine in <u>*Mr. Horn*</u> *(1979)*

VICTORY

One victory doesn't mean the ending of war.
Crazy Horse played by Victor Mature in <u>Chief Crazy Horse</u> (1955)

There are many ways to victory, and not all of them so violent.
Don Luis played by Gilbert Roland in <u>The Sacketts</u> (1979)

VIOLENCE

I can understand the violence of a storm. It's a natural thing not meant to harm anyone. But the violence of men, their cruelty and savageness to one another, to themselves!
The Preacher played by William Shatner in <u>The Outrage</u> (1964)

VIRTUE

According to the gospel of old Luke Matthews, virtue is its own punishment.
Luke Matthews played by James Coburn in <u>Bite the Bullet</u> (1975)

I was taught virtue was its own reward.
The Durango Kid/Bill Lowery played by Charles Starrett in <u>The Durango Kid</u> (1940)

VIRTUES & VICES

'Men's evil manners live in brass, their virtues in water.'
Sterling Mott played by Sandy McPeak, quoting Shakespeare, in <u>Independence</u> (1987)

VISION

If you look long enough, Miss Hayes, you might see things that aren't on a horizon.
Brett Wade played by Rory Calhoun in <u>Dawn at Socorro</u> (1954)

Never assume that because a man has no eyes he cannot see.
Master Po played by Keye Luke in <u>Kung Fu</u> (1972)

I know what I want and I know how to get it.
Wes Merritt played by Arthur Kennedy in <u>The Lusty Men</u> (1952)

A vision will help you realize your oneness with all things.
Wanagi played by Ron Soble in <u>The Mystic Warrior</u> (1984)

Buteo: What I see is that my course is clear. I see that there are times when you do what should be done. And there are times when you do what must be done. And it is never a clear choice. You do what you have to do.
Redeye: I love the way this guy talks!
Buteo played by Jimmie F. Skaggs and Redeye played by Andrew Divoff in <u>Oblivion</u> (1994)

What I see don't exist yet.
Woodrow F. Call played by Jon Voight in <u>Return to Lonesome Dove</u> (1993)

VOMITING

And try not to puke. You may have to lay in it for a long time.
John Russell played by Paul Newman in <u>Hombre</u> (1967)

VOTING

Did you ever figure how many votes it might get you next fall if people in town saw you ride in with a murderer across your saddle?
Marshal Dan Mitchell played by Randolph Scott in <u>Abilene Town</u> (1946)

You can fool some of the voters some of the time, but you can't fool all the voters most of the time.
George Peyton played by Grady Sutton in <u>Dudes Are Pretty People</u> (1942)

Ike: I only got beat by sixty votes.
Deputy: I meant to ask you, how many voters are there here?
Ike: Sixty-one.
Ike played by Cliff Edwards and Deputy Marshal Larry Durant played by Tim Holt in <u>Pirates of the Prairie</u> (1942)

WAITING

Waiting for someone is bad maybe, but it ain't as bad as having nobody to wait for.
Rachel Shaeffer played by Ann Dvorak in <u>The Secret of Convict Lake</u> (1951)

Those who learn to wait, win.
Mendoza played by Claudio Camaso in <u>Vengeance</u> (1968)

WANTS

If your wishes and wants are real enough, they'll come in search of you.
Celia Wallace played by Catherine Craig in <u>Albuquerque</u> (1948)

What you want and what you get are two different things.
Jeff Carter played by Eddie Acuff in <u>Guns of the Pecos</u> (1937)

I know the quickest way to make you want something is always to tell you that you can't have it.
Blackie Williams played by Ray Middleton in <u>Lady from Louisiana</u> (1941)

There is no place in this part of the country to waste your time crying over wants. Your life is about needs now.
Sarah Graham played by Theresa Russell in <u>Love Comes Softly</u> (2003)

Sometimes what a woman says she wants is a long walk from what she really wants.
Pearl played by Farrah Fawcett in <u>The Substitute Wife</u> (1994)

Everybody wants what he hasn't got.
Utah Blaine played by Rory Calhoun in <u>Utah Blaine</u> (1957)

WAR

Making money out of war is almost an act of nature.
Alvarez Kelly played by William Holden in <u>Alvarez Kelly</u> (1966)

I imagine God is weary of being called down on both sides of an argument.
Inman played by Jude Law in <u>Cold Mountain</u> (2003)

War changes people. They live on hate and revenge.
Major Clint Drango played by Jeff Chandler in <u>Drango</u> (1957)

Even in war, life goes on.
Mangas played by Ross Martin in <u>Geronimo</u> (1962)

It is well that war is so terrible or we should grow too fond of it.
General Robert E. Lee played by Robert Duvall in <u>Gods and Generals</u> (2003)

Captain: General, did you consider that a show of force now might start this war?
General: Or prevent it.
Captain Charles Wood played by Sam Elliott and General Oliver O. Howard played by James Whitmore in <u>I Will Fight No More Forever</u> (1975)

I have absolutely no romantic conceptions about the consequences of war.
Sam Houston played by Stacy Keach in <u>James A. Michener's Texas</u> (1995)

War is not going to go away because we don't talk about it.
Timothy Macahan played by Richard Kiley in <u>The Macahans</u> (1976)

The one who loses the war is always slower to forget.
Victor Renaud played by Dick Curtis in The Riders of the Northwest Mounted (1943)

War is not the answer. It's the road to self-destruction.
Man Called Horse/John Morgan played by Richard Harris in Triumphs of a Man Called Horse (1983)

They say a war makes a man grow up fast.
Jeanie Miller played by Karen Steele in Westbound (1959)

I'm home but I didn't leave the war. I brought it with me.
Jesse James played by Ray Stricklyn in Young Jesse James (1960)

WAR & DEATH

This is the dangerous time. Men start to smell victory and they get cautious. They resent having to die.
Lt. Hutton played by Scott Heindl in The Colt (2005)

We do not fear our own death, you and I. But there comes a time when we are never quite prepared for so many to die.
General Robert E. Lee played by Martin Sheen in Gettysburg (1993)

My religious belief teaches me to feel as safe in battle as in bed. God has fixed the time for my death. I do not concern myself with that, but to be always ready whenever it may overtake me.
General Stonewall Jackson played by Stephen Lang in Gods and Generals (2003)

Major: It's a shame we don't have more men to fight.
Colonel: Or less to die.
Major Duncan Heyward played by Henry Wilcoxon and Colonel Munro played by Hugh Buckler in The Last of the Mohicans (1936)

Isn't that what war is? It's murder! All wrapped up and sanctified with a flag.
Edward Janroe played by David Dukes in <u>Last Stand at Saber River</u> (1997)

WAR & PEACE

The words of his mouth were smoother than butter, but war was in his heart.
Juke played by George "Gabby" Hayes in <u>Albuquerque</u> (1948)

Making peace is a lot harder than making war.
Friend played by Simon Eine in <u>Another Man, Another Chance</u> (1977)

It takes two to call off a war.
Al Sieber played by John McIntire in <u>Apache</u> (1954)

What we have lost will never be returned to us. The land will not heal ... too much blood. My heart will not heal. All we can do is make peace with the past and try to learn from it.
Ada Monroe played by Nicole Kidman in <u>Cold Mountain</u> (2003)

It is not death we must talk about, but life. To fight a war means death to us. Only in peace can we live.
Chief Joseph played by Ned Romero in <u>I Will Fight No More Forever</u> (1975)

There's nothing as successful as a bullet between the eyes of an Apache to make him peaceful.
Captain Case McCloud played by George Montgomery in <u>Indian Uprising</u> (1952)

We must not let problems of war blind us to greater problems of the peace to come or we will have fought in vain.
Abraham Lincoln played by Charles Edward Bull in <u>The Iron Horse</u> (1924)

The Bible says, turn your armor into plowshares. But I say unto you, turn your plowshares into armor.
Ned Kelly played by Mick Jagger in <u>Ned Kelly</u> (1970)

Sometimes we must fight in order to find peace.
Koda played by Michael Beck in Triumphs of a Man Called Horse *(1983)*

WARNING

To be forewarned is to be forearmed.
Henry Blackstone played by Charles Evans in Twilight on the Rio Grande *(1947)*

WARRIORS

Every warrior hopes a good death will find him.
One Stab played by Gordon Tootoosis in Legends of the Fall *(1994)*

Warriors without war are soon people who cease to exist.
Micahpi played by Apollonia Kotero in The Mystic Warrior *(1984)*

There are many ways to be a great warrior.
Pocahontas played by Sandrine Holt in Pocahontas: The Legend *(1995)*

WATER

Water—man's greatest friend. But unleashed—man's greatest foe.
Prologue in Rovin' Tumbleweeds *(1939)*

WEAKNESS

Every man has his weak spot.
Rice Martin played by Lorne Greene in The Hard Man *(1957)*

WEAPONS

For faith and love are the strongest weapons in the world.
Rev. Alden played by Dabbs Greer in Little House: The Last Farewell *(1984)*

Ruby: Jesus wasn't unarmed. His weapons were compassion and mercy.
Ringo: What kind of weapons are them? A good six-shooter, that's what He should have had.
Ruby played by Lorella De Luca and Ringo played by Giuliano Gemma in A Pistol for Ringo (1965)

Violence is for fools. Wisdom is a better weapon.
Moy Soong played by Soo Yong in Secrets of the Wasteland (1941)

A weapon is only as good as the man who uses it.
Emperor Maximilian played by George Macready in Vera Cruz (1954)

WEBS

You're caught in a web of your own making. Instead of searching for a way out of it, you'd rather strangle in it.
Kate Hardison played by Marguerite Chapman in Coroner Creek (1948)

WEDDINGS

I've been to a lot of weddings in my time, Mr. Peale. But this is absolutely the most recent.
Buffalo Bill Cody played by Dennis Weaver in Lonesome Dove: Tales of the Plains (1992)

WEST

The West is where every child played cowboys and Indians.
Prologue in Gunslinger's Revenge (2005)

The West is a place on the map, not a way to live.
Jedediah Smith played by Josh Brolin in Into the West (2005)

There's nothing around here but scenery.
Kay Dodge played by June Storey in Rancho Grande (1940)

WHISKEY

God invented the whiskey to keep the Irish from ruling the world.
Rock Mullaney played by David O'Hara in <u>Crossfire Trail</u> *(2001)*

Nick the Bartender: And what will you have?
Ramirez: Whiskey and water.
Nick: I'm sorry, sir. We don't serve no fancy drinks here.
Nick the Bartender played by Billy Bevan and Ramirez played by Nelson Eddy in <u>The Girl of the Golden West</u> *(1938)*

Lord, but that does heal the aches of a loser.
Ace Bonner played by Robert Preston in <u>Junior Bonner</u> *(1972)*

I would not put a thief in my mouth to steal my brains.
Mattie Ross played by Kim Darby in <u>True Grit</u> *(1969)*

WHISKEY & WOMEN

Ain't you never learned the advantages of good whiskey and bad women?
Seely Jones played by Claude Akins in <u>A Distant Trumpet</u> *(1964)*

WHITE FLAGS

It don't seem exactly right to shoot a man waiving a white flag.
Grandpa played by James Barton in <u>Yellow Sky</u> *(1948)*

WHOREHOUSES

You'd think I was closing down the Alamo!
John O'Hanlan, played by James Stewart, commenting on public opinion on closing the whorehouse in <u>The Cheyenne Social Club</u> *(1970)*

WHORES

I'm crossing my legs for good.
Berle played by Lee Purcell in <u>Dirty Little Billy</u> *(1972)*

Woodrow: I reckon a man has got more to do than sit in a saloon with a whore.
Gus: Like what?
Captain Woodrow F. Call played by Tommy Lee Jones and Gus McCrae played by Robert Duvall in <u>Lonesome Dove</u> *(1989)*

WIDOWS

You've locked the gates on your emotions. You refuse to let yourself fall in love again. All because you're living in wedlock with a ghost.
Major Howell Brady played by Jeff Chandler in <u>War Arrow</u> *(1954)*

WILDNESS

They say that a wild plant never lives very long indoors.
Elaine Corwin played by Maureen O'Hara in <u>War Arrow</u> *(1954)*

WILLS

I never had read a will that pleased a woman.
Judge Town played by William Fawcett in <u>Tumbleweed Trail</u> *(1946)*

WINDMILLS

A man must not fight windmills.
Pancho Villa played by Antonio Banderas in <u>And Starring Pancho Villa as Himself</u> *(2003)*

WINNERS & LOSERS

We got a problem. We both can't win. Oh, that's not the problem. The problem is, I can't afford to lose.
Luke Matthews played by James Coburn in <u>Bite the Bullet</u> *(1975)*

You got to face losing as well as winning.
Chris Danning played by Randolph Scott in <u>Coroner Creek</u> *(1948)*

Deputy: If two men disagree around here, they shoot it out.

Sheriff: Yeah, that's right.

Deputy: If the winner is justified, we make him a deputy. If he's wrong, we hang him.

Deputy Lafe Walters played by Skeeter Bill Robbins and Sheriff Matt Verity played by Al Bridge in Cowboy Counsellor (1932)

Goodfellow: I can't understand why I never win!

Holliday: You don't play very well. Besides that, you never cheat.

Dr. Charles Goodfellow played by Karl Swenson and Doc Holliday played by Jason Robards, Jr., in Hour of the Gun (1967)

Ace: If the world is all about winners, what's for the losers?

Junior: Well, somebody's got to hold the horses, Ace.

Ace Bonner played by Robert Preston and Junior Bonner played by Steve McQueen in Junior Bonner (1972)

They've won but that doesn't mean that you've lost.

Susan Larrabee played by Fay McKenzie in Sierra Sue (1941)

The only thing worse than a bad loser is a bad winner.

Steve played by John Savage in The Virginian (1999)

When you stand to win, you got to be able to stand to lose.

Johnny Gannon played by Richard Widmark in Warlock (1959)

WISDOM

The mountain lion is wise. He avoids grizzly bear.

Hawk played by Pato Hoffmann in Cheyenne Warrior (1994)

A wise old owl sat in an oak. The more he heard, the less he spoke. The less he spoke, the more he heard. Now wasn't that a wise old bird?

Eula Goodnight played by Katharine Hepburn in Rooster Cogburn (1975)

As our Chinese friends say: 'He who acknowledges ignorance is on the road to wisdom.'
J.C. Crane played by Robert Warwick in <u>Sugarfoot</u> (1951)

I reckon it's just a case of too soon old and too late smart.
Will Penny played by Charlton Heston in <u>Will Penny</u> (1968)

When I was young like you, my son, I said many things. Now that I am old, I have many scars to show for my quick words.
Red Calf played by Ace Powell in <u>Winterhawk</u> (1976)

WITNESSES
The dead sometimes tell more than the living.
Sheriff Thompson played by Forbes Murray in <u>The Dead Don't Dream</u> (1948)

WIVES
No man can take another man's wife away from him unless she wants to be taken.
Lucy Summerton played by Karen Steele in <u>Decision at Sundown</u> (1957)

I've been told that a good wife hears only what her husband wants her to hear.
Brice Chamberlain played by Melvyn Douglas in <u>The Sea of Grass</u> (1947)

My wife, she's so mean she barks at the dogs.
Fiesta played by Akim Tamiroff in <u>Union Pacific</u> (1939)

WOMEN
Women bury their dead and keep on living.
Captain Rod Douglas played by George Peppard in <u>Cannon for Cordoba</u> (1970)

I read a book once that said that women always look their best in the peace and quiet that follows a storm of violence.
Tom Destry, Jr., played by James Stewart in <u>Destry Rides Again</u> (1939)

Every time I've ever tried to figure out a woman, I wished I hadn't even tried.
Brady Hawkes played by Kenny Rogers in <u>The Gambler: The Adventure Continues</u> (1983)

Nice women can ruin a town.
Ned Trent played by John Hodiak in <u>The Harvey Girls</u> (1946)

I've seen women I'd look at quicker but never one I'd look at longer.
Candy Johnson played by Clark Gable in <u>Honky Tonk</u> (1941)

Rifles and women don't mix.
Tobias Taylor played by Chill Wills in <u>Kentucky Rifle</u> (1956)

You're no woman! You're a money machine!
Winchester Jack played by Charles Southwood in <u>Roy Colt & Winchester Jack</u> (1970)

Cherry is like a sleek yacht or thoroughbred horse: exciting, beautiful, but hard to handle.
Roy Glennister played by Jeff Chandler in <u>The Spoilers</u> (1955)

WORDS

Some things better be left unsaid.
Gabby Whittaker played by George "Gabby" Hayes in <u>Along the Navajo Trail</u> (1945)

Sometimes the right word from the right person helps more than medicine.
Luther Mason played by Warner Anderson in <u>Bad Bascomb</u> (1946)

Sometimes you cram more sense into a few words than you'd find in a whole shelf of philosophy.
Eaton played by Robert Coote in <u>Bad Lands</u> (1939)

You don't say much but you get your point across.
Cassie played by Linda Cardellini in <u>Brokeback Mountain</u> (2005)

It would be a poor world if a kind word came with an obligation attached.
Tom Covington played by Darcy Belsher in <u>The Colt</u> (2005)

I ain't ever seen soft words stop Comanche arrows yet.
Jason Clay played by Lance Fuller in <u>Kentucky Rifle</u> (1956)

Sticks and stones will break my bones, but words will never hurt me.
Buckshot Peters played by Wally Vernon in <u>Outlaws of Santa Fe</u> (1944)

Just saying a good thing don't make it so.
Uncle Famous Prill played by Juano Hernandez in <u>Stars in My Crown</u> (1950)

Unkind remarks are like bullets. Once fired, being sorry don't stop the damage.
Robert "Buck" Sawyer played by Tom Keene in <u>Sundown Trail</u> (1931)

WORK

You got to break eggs to make a cake.
Sheriff Masters played by Ted Adams in <u>Billy the Kid Trapped</u> (1942)

No one ever drowned in sweat or was buried in blisters.
Dale Weems played by Ted Danson in <u>Cowboy</u> (1983)

Collins: You're fired! Understand? Fired!
Tom: Well, if that's the way you feel about it, I quit.
Collins played by Frank LaRue and Tom Devlin played by Buck Jones in <u>Forbidden Trail</u> (1932)

Do your own dirty work.
Cam Bleeker played by Fess Parker in <u>The Jayhawkers</u> (1959)

What the job is ain't important. It's how you do it.
Lyedecker played by Jim Brown in <u>100 Rifles</u> (1969)

You don't get lard unless you boil the hog.
Colleen McCloud played by Melissa Sue Anderson in <u>The Return of Sam McCloud</u> *(1989)*

There's never been a man that got rich working on a salary.
Wyatt Earp played by Kevin Costner in <u>Wyatt Earp</u> *(1994)*

WORTH

A man's worth has got nothing to do with money.
Sam Kendrick played by Stacy Keach in <u>Desolation Canyon</u> *(2006)*

It wouldn't be worth having if it came too easy.
Lash LaRue played himself in <u>Frontier Revenge</u> *(1948)*

Anything worth having is worth earning.
Hopalong Cassidy played by William Boyd in <u>The Frontiersmen</u> *(1938)*

The only way I could ever tell how much a thing was worth was by how bad I wanted it.
Jeff McCloud played by Robert Mitchum in <u>The Lusty Men</u> *(1952)*

WOUNDS

Bullets aren't the only thing that can tear you apart. Disappointment and people can smash you too.
Ted Wallace played by Russell Hayden in <u>Albuquerque</u> *(1948)*

Some wounds time just don't heal.
Jonas Steele played by Stacy Keach in <u>The Blue and the Gray</u> *(1982)*

Blame keeps wounds open; only forgiveness heals them.
Ivar played by Tom Aldredge in <u>O Pioneers!</u> *(1992)*

WRONG

Your record is perfect. You're wrong again!
Mike Prescott played by Forrest Tucker in <u>California Passage</u> *(1950)*

XENOPHOBIA

There's only one kind of people I don't like: strangers.
Mama Malone played by Ruth Springford in <u>5 Card Stud</u> *(1968)*

White eyes kill what they fear.
Running Dog played by Raoul Trujillo in <u>Black Fox: Blood Horse</u> *(1995)*

YOUTH

It is natural for the young to forget the old.
Felipe Gonzales played by Martin Garralaga in <u>The Big Sombrero</u> *(1949)*

According to the words of the song, we're promised a city of gold in the hereafter. I used to think that was a long time to have to wait. But I know now

that there is a city of gold right here on earth for everyone of us: the city of our youth.
Narration by Marshall Thompson in <u>Stars in My Crown</u> *(1950)*

YOUTHFUL OFFENDERS

I buried a lot of friends who thought fuzzy-faced kids weren't dangerous.
Chris played by Lee Van Cleef in <u>The Magnificent Seven Ride!</u> *(1972)*

ZEN

Kwai Chang: What happens in a man's life has already been written. A man must move through life as his destiny wills.

Han Fei: Yes, yet each man is free to live as he chooses. Though they seem opposite, both are true.

Kwai Chang Caine played by David Carradine and Han Fei played by Benson Fong in Kung Fu (1972)

Sheriff: It is said that a moth that lives too close to the flame leads a short life.

Kwai Chang: But in China it is said, 'There is little difference between a long life and a short one. Both are but moments in time.'

Sheriff Mills played by Luke Askew and Kwai Chang Caine played by David Carradine in Kung Fu: The Movie (1986)

ZIP CODE

I ain't going no place until I know where I'm going.

Sgt. "Bar" Barstow played by Wallace Beery in The Man from Dakota (1940)

Vic: Where can we go?

Barbara: Anywhere.

Vic: That's the same as nowhere.

Vic Hansbro played by Arthur Kennedy and Barbara Waggoman played by Cathy O'Donnell in The Man from Laramie (1955)

ZORRO

This Zorro comes upon you like a graveyard ghost; and like a ghost, he disappears.

The Henchman was uncredited in The Mark of Zorro (1920)

Zorro has been dead these many years. But the spirit of Zorro will never die.

James Vega/Zorro played by John Carroll in Zorro Rides Again (1937)

AFTERWORD

Hardy: Is that true?

Jedediah: If it isn't, it ought to be.

Hardy Fimps played by Clay O'Brien and Jedediah Nightlinger played by Roscoe Lee Browne in The Cowboys (1972)

See you at trail's end!

Aud Niven played by Janice Rule in Gun for a Coward (1957)

Come on, Luke! We got a sunset to catch!

Roger Miller was voice of Jolly Jumper, the Horse, in Lucky Luke (1991)

Clint: I'll be looking back for you all the way.

Lilly: And I'll be looking ahead for you.

Clint McDonald played by John Ireland and Lilly played by Joanne Dru in Southwest Passage (1954)

And that's the way it really happened, give or take a lie or two.

Epilogue in Sunset (1988)

May the Good Spirit be with you.

Tianay played by Anne Bancroft in Walk the Proud Land (1956)

INDEX

MOVIE TITLES

T

ACKNOWLEDGMENTS

Although the quotations covered in this book are uttered by actors and actresses portraying frontier characters, I want to make it crystal clear and acknowledge that it is the writers of these sagebrushers who are the real voices and heroes, and this book would not be possible without them.

I have taped over 1,800 westerns and rented or borrowed another 200 cowboy movies. I have personally reviewed and categorized all the quotations contained in this book.

I wish to acknowledge the tremendous support, guidance, and direction I received from agent Rita Rosenkranz (New York); publisher Ruina Judd (Texas); editor Dixie Nixon (Arizona); and book designer Isabel Lasater Hernandez (Texas), who made this book come together. Any errors were certainly unintentional and are my responsibility.

BRIGHT SKY PRESS
Box 416
Albany, Texas 76430

Library of Congress Cataloging-in-Publication Data

Western movie wit and wisdom / [compiled] by Jim Kane.
        p. cm.
    Includes bibliographical references and index.
    ISBN 978-1-931721-97-4 (jacketed hardcover : alk. paper) 1. Western
films—Quotations, maxims, etc. I. Kane, Jim, 1946– II. Title.

PN1995.9.W4 W37
791.43'6278—dc22

                                                          2007000285

Cover art © Hatch Show Print, Nashville, Tennessee
Design and topic illustrations by Isabel Lasater Hernandez
Edited by Dixie Nixon
Printed in China through Asia Pacific Offset